BRITISH AUTHORS

Introductory Critical Studies

General Editor: ROBIN MAYHEAD

WILLIAM BLAKE

In this series

John Keats by ROBIN MAYHEAD
William Wordsworth by GEOFFREY DURRANT
George Eliot by R. T. JONES
Jane Austen by YASMINE GOONERATNE

WILLIAM BLAKE

BY

D. G. GILLHAM

Professor of English
University of Cape Town

CAMBRIDGE
AT THE UNIVERSITY PRESS
1973

Published by the Syndics of the Cambridge University Press
Bentley House, 200 Euston Road, London NW1 2DB
American Branch: 32 East 57th Street, New York, N.Y. 10022

© Cambridge University Press 1973

Library of Congress Catalogue Card Number: 72–80296

ISBNs:
0 521 08680 9 hard covers
0 521 09735 5 paperback

Printed in Great Britain
by W & J Mackay Limited, Chatham

GENERAL PREFACE

This study of William Blake is the fifth in a series of short introductory critical studies of the more important British authors. The aim of the series is to go straight to the authors' works; to discuss them directly with a maximum of attention to concrete detail; to say what they are and what they do, and to indicate a valuation. The general critical attitude implied in the series is set out at some length in my *Understanding Literature*. Great literature is taken to be to a large extent self-explanatory to the reader who will attend carefully enough to what it says. 'Background' study, whether biographical or historical, is not the concern of the series.

It is hoped that this approach will suit a number of kinds of reader, in particular the general reader who would like an introduction which talks about the works themselves; and the student who would like a general critical study as a starting point, intending to go on to read more specialized works later. Since 'background' is not erected as an insuperable obstacle, readers in other English-speaking countries, countries where English is a second language, or even those for whom English is a foreign language, should find the books helpful. In Britain and the Commonwealth, students and teachers in universities and in the higher forms of secondary schools will find that the authors chosen for treatment are those most often prescribed for study in public and university examinations.

The series could be described as an attempt to make available to a wide public the results of the literary criticism of the last thirty years, and especially the methods associated with Cambridge. If the result is an increase in the reading, with enjoyment and understanding, of the great works of English literature, the books will have fulfilled their wider purpose.

ROBIN MAYHEAD

CONTENTS

INTRODUCTION

The first six chapters of this book are devoted to Blake's *Songs of Innocence and of Experience*, and these chapters are based on a longer work by the present author: *Blake's Contrary States* (Cambridge, 1966). In chapter 7 some general observations are made on Blake's style of writing in his longer poems as well as in the shorter works, and a more detailed discussion of *The Marriage of Heaven and Hell* is given. Chapters 8 and 9 are each devoted to a single work, the chapter on the *Visions of the Daughters of Albion* being an adaptation of an article that appeared in *The Wascana Review* (Regina, Canada, Spring 1969, pp. 41ff).

Nearly all Blake's writings were printed and issued by himself. He was an engraver by trade, and etched the plates from which he reproduced his books, the text being accompanied by illustrations which are an integral part of the work and help elucidate the meaning. The text of the *Songs of Innocence and of Experience* used here is taken from a facsimile edition edited by Sir Geoffrey Keynes and published by Rupert Hart-Davis in 1967. The text of *Visions of the Daughters of Albion* is also taken from a facsimile edition, issued by Dent in 1932. The punctuation in Blake's editions is not always clear, and he seems to have been careless in making his commas, which often look like full stops. It is usual to edit the punctuation in printed texts, but this might have the effect of imposing on the poems a meaning not intended by the poet, so the punctuation is given here as it appears in the two facsimile reproductions. All other Blake quotations are taken from the Nonesuch edition of 1957, edited by Geoffrey Keynes.

Most space is given, in this work, to an examination of the *Songs*. These short poems are the most easily understood of Blake's writings, and they are essential to an understanding of the poet, as well as being the most important of his works. What these poems lack in length, they make up in quality; they are Blake's best work, and after writing them he progressively lapsed into the strained, obscure and abstract manner that makes the long poems unsatisfactory to many readers. In chapter 7, this tendency is examined in some detail, and the examination continued in chapters 8 and 9.

The *Songs* are difficult, despite the simplicity of their style and diction. They have been variously interpreted and, as the analysis given in the pages that follow has no warrant of general acceptance, it is only proper that, at the outset, the writer should give, in outline, his basic assumptions, distinguishing them from those made by other writers. It is assumed here that the *Songs of Innocence* and the *Songs of Experience* were conceived by Blake as an artistic whole, and that his intention was that the two sets of songs should be read together and contrasted with each other. As Blake states on the combined title page, the poems are to be read as 'Shewing the Two Contrary States of the Human Soul'. The one state, presumably, may be better understood by referring to its contrary. On pp. 145–6 it is argued that though a period of five years separated the publication of the two series we have no conclusive evidence to fix the dates of composition, and there is no reason for not taking them together.

A second assumption is that the poems are composed 'dramatically' – that Blake does not speak in his own voice, or even through the mouth of an imagined character (a child for instance) in order to give his own impressions, but that he is detached in the same way that a playwright is detached from the persons in his play. It is often stated that the two series give us Blake's impressions at different periods of his life (at the ages of thirty-two and thirty-seven) and that the difference in feeling between the sets shows that the poet had undergone a change of heart. It is here assumed, on grounds which will be made clear, that Blake is examining his speakers from outside, constructing a series of character studies in order to demonstrate a range of human potentialities, but that none of these should be taken as directly representative of the poet. They may be indirectly representative of Blake for the reason that all character analysis is, to some degree, a reflection of what the writer finds latent in his own soul, but Blake's primary aim is not self-expression. The poems are psychological studies but also they are critical; Blake is not so far detached from the states he puts on show that he does not judge them, and we are meant to see some speakers as admirable, others as confused, selfish, and so on, but the reader must help to make the assessments. Blake's judgements are implicit in the poems, but not obvious.

A third assumption made here is that Blake's later works do not help us in the interpretation of the *Songs*. It seems wrong to take the Prophecies, which are difficult and obscure, as a key to the *Songs*, which are less difficult and fairly lucid. Critics who apply this method of interpretation, it is true, assume that the Prophecies are fully and finally understood, but such certitude, which would be dangerous enough in the face of any work of literature, is quite reckless in the case of such mysterious works as these. It is indicative of error that such critics arbitrarily apply a fixed symbolic significance, culled from the Prophecies, to the images found in the *Songs*. But Blake was an artist writing poetry, not a constructor of crossword puzzles with clues to be solved by research. His words and images come alive in the context of the poems, their significance varies from one poem to another, and it is the test of the reader that he should be sensitive to these variations. Indeed, the key to these poems is to see that the 'Contrary States' recognize the same objects and experiences differently. Quite apart from this special intention in the *Songs*, however, it is the hallmark of any good poem that it breathes its own life into the symbols it uses, and if it could be demonstrated that Blake's symbols were arbitrary and static we should be forced to conclude that his poems were of little value. As his poems are explained by those critics who make the assumption of fixed symbolic significance, it is, indeed, possible to conclude that the poet is hardly worth reading, and the same observation holds good for those critics who interpret the *Songs* in terms of a body of occult knowledge in which Blake is supposed to have been an initiate. The *Songs* are not proof of a dogmatic gift in their writer, however, but of an imaginative one, and they are valuable for the flexibility and freshness of their thought. Blake's symbolism is discussed at various points in the following work (pp. 11ff, for instance), and his use of symbols derived from occult sources is discussed in chapter 8.

I

INNOCENT JOY

The reader, seriously studying the *Songs* for the first time, soon becomes aware that, when read together, the poems make an impression unlike that received from examples scattered in anthologies. Each poem makes good sense on its own, but one feels also that there is a purpose in their being brought together and, as the sense of the individual poems is more thoroughly explored, the unifying purpose is gradually made clear. The first intimation of this larger intention usually comes with the observation that many of the poems are explicitly paired. There are, for instance, two *Holy Thursdays*, one in *Songs of Innocence* and one in *Songs of Experience*. It is a short step to discover that nearly all the poems have their counterparts – that *The Sick Rose* of Experience may be read with *The Blossom* of Innocence, *The Tyger* with *The Lamb*, and so on. At first, the reader resists the connexion – he knows that poems must be granted their autonomy if they are to be read successfully; he has been warned not to import irrelevant information or speculation not disciplined by the work in hand. Soon, however, he realizes that Blake's contrasts are helpful, not because the one poem adds to the other, but because the reader's mind, in possession of both poems, is better able to discern what each contains. In studying *Infant Sorrow*, for example, one's speculations are more likely to take the relevant direction if the innocent counterpart, *Infant Joy*, is borne in mind.

INFANT SORROW

My mother groand! my father wept.
Into the dangerous world I leapt:
Helpless. naked. piping loud:
Like a fiend hid in a cloud.

Struggling in my fathers hands:
Striving against my swadling bands:
Bound and weary I thought best
To sulk upon my mothers breast.

INFANT JOY

I have no name
I am but two days old –
What shall I call thee?
I happy am
Joy is my name. –
Sweet joy befall thee!

Pretty joy!
Sweet joy but two days old.
Sweet joy I call thee:
Thou dost smile.
I sing the while
Sweet joy befall thee.

Confronted by either of these poems singly, one's reaction might be to say: 'How true a representation of babyhood!' Reading them together, one is forced to add: 'How different the representations are!' *Infant Sorrow* is spoken in the first person, and it is his own entry to the world that the speaker describes. He draws on his observations of the behaviour of infants and interprets their gestures to show that the baby is aware of the hostility he must encounter in the world, and the resistance he must make in one form or another. The birth is a dire struggle for both mother and child and, once free, the infant, alarmed and blindly assertive, is ready to do battle – he 'leaps' into the world as though already alarmed, and strains against the opposition of his 'fathers hands' and the 'swadling bands' imposed upon him by a world that is 'dangerous'. He is 'a fiend hid in a cloud' – beneath the soft, rounded exterior of the babe not as yet formed and individual, is a tense, fiendishly obstinate will to oppose, so the convulsive movements of the child and his persistent cries are seen as ineffective attempts to have his own way and as utterances of unyielding protest. Even when resting, the baby has merely changed his tactics or is biding his time until his strength is greater. The child quietly feeding at his mother's breast is seen as temporarily beaten, 'bound and weary', but able to 'think best' to his own advantage, realizing that he is powerless at the moment. The pouting, frowning expression of the sucking child is interpreted, in the last line, as indicative of the frustration and resentment he feels while deliberately assuming a passive rôle.

Babies have various moods, we view them differently as our own moods vary, and different persons have different ideas of babyhood. For all these reasons, perhaps, *Infant Joy* presents another picture of the infant. The speaker, most probably the mother, does not conduct an introspective monologue, as in *Infant Sorrow*, but companionably makes up an imaginary conversation with her child, providing the responses herself, and probably touching his cheek in order to cause him to 'smile'. She projects her own contentment in interpreting the conduct of the babe, causes him to name himself 'Joy', describes him as happy in his own being ('I happy am') and as a source of joy to herself. The experienced speaker found no joy in his babe and predicted none for the future, but the innocent mother is convinced of the joyous nature of her child and blesses it at the end of each stanza with the hope that the future will be joyous too. 'Sweet joy befall thee' is the refrain to her song, though in giving this benediction the mother does not regard joy as inevitable, only as a possibility she wishes for her child. In expressing herself in this way she shows herself less dogmatic than the speaker in *Infant Sorrow*, who sees life only as a tense struggle against opposition.

There are other ways in which the innocent mother shows herself to be less dogmatic than the experienced speaker. The latter cannot possibly recall the event he describes, but he can draw on his generalizations to interpret the actions of any baby, even unknown ones. Put another way: the sight of any baby is an occasion for the reassertion of a settled conviction that life is a battle. All situations, no doubt, afford the speaker evidence that he is right in holding this view. The innocent mother also projects herself into the baby; she cannot know his inner feelings, and it is un-likely that a two-day-old infant feels anything that an adult could recognize. But she has more freedom than the experienced speaker, for the feeling she projects is the outcome of an immediate situa-tion and her attitude towards the child is conceived in relation to him as an individual close to her. She is so immersed in the present circumstance that she has forgotten her pains experienced only two days ago (line 2), while the experienced speaker, concerned with a theoretical situation, insists on the groans he cannot have been aware of (line 1).

The minds of the innocent and experienced speakers take different directions and we can see this more clearly when we con-trast them. The style of speaking in each poem also helps empha-size the difference – *Infant Sorrow* is a monologue and is metrically more formal to suit the fixed ideas that underlie the description, while *Infant Joy* is a dialogue in form, and has short irregular lines and a simple unaffectedly repetitive diction to suit the spontaneity of a momentary feeling. The experienced speaker gives a most forceful description of the ineffectual vigour of the child, whose 'piping loud' is both weak and insistent; who can 'struggle' though small enough to be contained in the hands of his adversary (line 5), and 'strive' when bound tight prisoner. But, however fine his description, the intelligence of the narrator is turned inward – his description fits his theory, and only if we accept his theory can we regard the description as altogether true. The intelligence of the mother is turned outward because she is making a spontaneous reaction to a real circumstance. The delight which colours her description is properly a part of the occasion described and we can accept the description without qualification. The two poems present us with two conceptions of the truth about babies. The experienced poem is primarily concerned with babyhood in the abstract, also with the expression of a settled idea of the human condition, and it brings these abstruse notions very vigoroysly to light in the particular description it gives. We might label the speaker's description of the infant as 'fanciful' because it gives expression to his habits of mind. The innocent mother is concerned with her baby at a particular moment and she, too, 'makes up' a rôle for her child. But what she 'makes up' is a consequence of her present delight and the affection induced by the presence of her baby. Her settled notions of babyhood, whatever they may be, are not given expression, and we might say that her description of the child is 'imaginative' because her mind and her circumstance affect each other in determining what she perceives.

Infant Joy and *Infant Sorrow* are vigorous expressions of the human mind exercised in distinct ways, and Blake deepens our appreciation of this distinction as we explore contrary poems. A very similar contrast is found between *The Tyger* from *Songs of Experience* and *The Lamb* from *Songs of Innocence* which explore, each in its own way, our notions of the Deity. Blake knew that God can come to men only as they are capable of receiving him, and so the speakers in the two poems have quite different notions of the divine nature.

The Tyger

Tyger Tyger. burning bright,
In the forests of the night:
What immortal hand or eye.
Could frame thy fearful symmetry?

In what distant deeps or skies.
Burnt the fire of thine eyes?
On what wings dare he aspire?
What the hand, dare sieze the fire?

And what shoulder. & what art.
Could twist the sinews of thy heart?
And when thy heart began to beat.
What dread hand? & what dread feet?

What the hammer? what the chain,
In what furnace was thy brain?
What the anvil? what dread grasp.
Dare its deadly terrors clasp?

When the stars threw down their spears
And water'd heaven with their tears:
Did he smile his work to see?
Did he who made the Lamb make thee?

Tyger Tyger burning bright,
In the forests of the night:
What immortal hand or eye.
Dare frame thy fearful symmetry?

The Lamb

Little Lamb who made thee
Dost thou know who made thee
Gave thee life & bid thee feed.
By the stream & o'er the mead:
Gave thee clothing of delight.
Softest clothing wooly bright;
Gave thee such a tender voice,
Making all the vales rejoice:
Little Lamb who made thee
Dost thou know who made thee

Little Lamb, I'll tell thee.
Little Lamb I'll tell thee;
He is called by thy name.
For he calls himself a Lamb:
He is meek & he is mild,
He became a little child:
I a child & thou a lamb.
We are called by his name.
Little Lamb God bless thee
Little Lamb God bless thee

The shock experienced in the presence of the Tyger causes the speaker to look farther than the world he knows – to the 'distant deeps or skies' beyond comprehensible space. The beast is part of the creation, but its beauty and ferocity have overwhelmed the mind; there is no possibility of accepting the creature in the comfortable manner made possible by habit, and its appearance makes the accustomed world take on mysterious and frightening dimensions. The Tyger is 'burning bright', a clearly distinguished, vigorous and dangerous presence, vividly itself in a place that is vast, gloomy and mysterious, the unexpected strangeness of the fierce animal having caused the universe it inhabits to become an incomprehensible place where the secrets of nature are hidden in a silent gloom of 'night' and 'forest'. The mind of the speaker is forced to explore a realm where his senses cannot assist him. He asks questions, though he cannot hope for any answers and cannot know, even, if his questions are the relevant ones. The overwhelming fact of the Tyger causes him to probe ultimate things though he can only conceive of the creator dimly, in human terms, and of the creation as the performance of an artisan of wonderful skill and strength. He knows that he cannot know – that he can only guess – and so extends his imagination to picture the process in the most lively way he can, though that picture must leave the mystery unsolved. Even the stars, first of all created things, having knowledge that must be superhuman – even they are struck with grief and horror when they first view this new creature; they 'water heaven with their tears' and, unable to understand the purpose of the creator, 'throw down their spears' in astonishment and despair. If the creator smiled (and the speaker can only wonder if he did) it cannot be known why. Perhaps it was because the devouring Tyger satisfied his cruel nature, perhaps because in his greater wisdom he saw a place for the Tyger in his creation. The speaker does not know, even, if the same great being made both the Lamb and the Tyger, and there is a possibility, suggested in the second stanza, that the maker might be a subordinate being using materials taken with great daring from remote and dangerous parts of an already existent universe.

The creator cannot even be described. He has 'wings' and 'hands' and 'feet', but we never see him, only his operative members as the spectator's sight is held in fascinated attention by the details of the immense process being carried forward. We see the 'shoulder' exerting its strength, the 'hand' in control of its materials and the 'feet' of the craftsman as he moves about his work, but are too spell-bound to take in the scene as a whole. The Tyger is 'twisted' and forged into being under great force, appropriate to so fierce and implacable an animal, and as the beast takes shape the tension becomes greater, the questions are broken off in mid-sentence and the questioner speaks in breathless gasps of wonder until the process is complete at the end of the fourth stanza.

The description of the maker at work is a reflection of the effect of the Tyger on the speaker. The strength and the terrifying beauty of the animal are transferred to the description of its creation. We never lose awareness of the animal, though in the course of the poem there is a slight shift in perspective away from the beast and towards the mystery of its creator. In the first stanza the speaker asks:

> What immortal hand or eye.
> Could frame thy fearful symmetry?

The ability of the maker must be wonderful because his creature is so wonderful. It has 'symmetry' – a form we see as being right, though we cannot explain why it should be just so. In the last stanza the speaker wonders what god could 'Dare frame' the fearful symmetry. We are still aware of the terrible beauty of the animal but are more concerned than before with the inexplicable mystery of the mind and purpose of the creator himself, if the word 'mind' can adequately indicate an attribute of his being.

The Tyger is cast in the form of a series of unanswerable questions, while *The Lamb* gives confident answers. Even the questions in the first stanza are put rhetorically by the child, who speaks in order that he may make the replies he is sure are correct. It is, perhaps, because the speaker is a child that he is not concerned with distant or ultimate things. He knows who the maker is but does not think of the mystery of creation or the ineffable mind of the creator. Life has been given and he is concerned with the gift he knows, emphasizing the generosity of God by repeating the word 'gave'. His mind is occupied with the present actuality of the Lamb and with the actualities of his own protected existence.

8

He knows only the benign aspect of life – is familiar with the gentle Lamb, but not with the Tyger which destroys, and knows the creator as a loving being who is fully understandable by men because he 'became a little child' and lived as a man. Christ is called by the name of the Lamb, and Lamb and child are called by his name, because the names all connote the meek and mild gentleness, the 'Mercy, Pity, Peace and Love' known to all three beings. What the child has been told makes sense to him and he accepts that God is in sympathy with his creation, and takes on man's nature. The mystery of the creation is not considered and God's present love is implicitly accepted.

Blake's two poems present us with two different states of mind: that of the adult who is aware of the beauty and terror of the Tyger and of the imponderable questions suggested by its existence, and that of the child, serene in his simple appreciation and knowledge. The reader is tempted to say of the child that he can adopt the attitude he does because the knowledge he has is incomplete – children are not aware of the 'realities' of life, and so are able to accept naïve explanations of existence, whereas the adult must confront the harsh 'realities' of a world where weaker forms of life are devoured by the stronger. But both the child of *The Lamb* and the adult of *The Tyger* are realists in their own way. The child's experience may be limited, but he does not attempt to go beyond that experience to explain his world, and he has accepted the story of a gentle Jesus because it is consistent with the care and affection he knows. The adult would like to know more. His God is incomprehensible, but *The Tyger*, while it asserts this, cannot help making an attempt to reduce him to comprehensible form. Theologically, *The Tyger* is a reflection of the bafflement of the speaker, though it must be added that the bafflement is grounded on a real and vivid experience – the shock of encountering the Tyger itself. The child is aware only in terms of his protected existence, but the adult speaker is aware, for the moment, only of exposure in a world where bewilderment is checked by wonder. Both poems show reverence, each in its own way, the reverence being based, in each case, on the realities of the speaker's life.

In *The Lamb* and *The Tyger* Blake contrasts a child's simple faith
with the perplexed speculations of an adult, but it would be a mistake to assume that the tenor of the songs is to differentiate between
the mind that is childishly incomplete and the mature one that is
aware of complex problems. Blake's innocents are not always children and his children are not always innocent. The songs which may
be paired as contrasts generally present speakers in the same condition of life and the juxtaposition of child and adult is unusual.
It is unusual, also, for the experienced and innocent minds both to
be presented sympathetically, as they are in *The Lamb* and *The
Tyger*. More commonly, Blake's attitude towards Experience
seems to be that the state is inevitable but not admirable, and in
subsequent chapters we will examine his criticism of the state.
In *The Tyger* as in *Infant Sorrow*, however, the perceptions of the
speaker are vigorous and there are other *Songs of Experience* where
this is so. In *The Sick Rose*, for instance, the speaker seems to be
limited by an experienced, horrified view of all things sexual,
especially when we contrast the poem with the purity and tenderness expressed in *The Blossom* of the *Songs of Innocence*. The
experienced speaker, however, is not really limited by his experienced repugnance, as would at first appear.

THE SICK ROSE

O Rose thou art sick.
The invisible worm.
That flies in the night
In the howling storm:

Has found out thy bed
Of crimson joy:
And his dark secret love
Does thy life destroy.

THE BLOSSOM

Merry Merry Sparrow
Under leaves so green

A happy Blossom
Sees you swift as arrow
Seek your cradle narrow
Near my Bosom.

Pretty Pretty Robin
Under leaves so green
A happy Blossom
Hears you sobbing sobbing
Pretty Pretty Robin
Near my Bosom.

When a poet uses simile or metaphor he directly or indirectly compares one thing to another in a way that deepens our understanding of his subject. These two poems are not metaphorical, but symbolic; no comparison is apparent, we are not told directly what the subject of the poem may be though the poet has a subject clearly in mind or at the back of his mind, and the reader is challenged to interpret the significance of the symbolism. Such interpretation will probably not lead to a complete or even very satisfying statement of the subject (if that were possible the poet need not have chosen to write in this manner) but it does require an attempt to respond with the movements of the mind and deeper movements of the soul appropriate to the words used. Even in his most symbolic writings Blake does have an idea clearly in mind, though the idea may be very complex and be deeply rooted. In the case of these two poems the idea is sexual, the subject of the poems sexual intercourse and, as might be expected with such a theme, the roots go down to dark regions of our being – regions not easy to expose to the light.

We glimpse very dark realms of the mind in *The Sick Rose*. The male 'worm' and female 'Rose', which have 'Freudian' significance, give rise in the speaker to the half-hidden feelings of indecency, guilt and fear so easily associated with sexual experiences, especially in the mind of the adolescent, half-fascinated and half-repelled by a subject that has attracted so many prohibitions and superstitions. The worm is 'invisible', a hidden, groping and repulsive thing that 'flies in the night', choosing to work furtively, partly in shame, perhaps, but also partly in the self-gratification of a 'dark secret love' that delights in destruction. He goes intently and persistently to work like a nocturnal predator or some malignant being until he has 'found out' his object which he infects. He is associated, also, with the 'howling storm', a chaotic and bestial emotional crisis going on about him while he takes his dark flight.

Contrast the innocent poem. The Blossom, like the Rose, is feminine and she addresses the male part, first as a Sparrow and then, when he changes, as a Robin. In the experienced poem, the sexual encounter is described from the outside, the Rose is addressed in the second person and a diagnosis made of her condition. The innocent poem admits us to the feelings of the Blossom, who utters her contentment, being a 'happy Blossom' in both stanzas, not 'sick' or remorseful after the event. She admires the male without fear, revulsion of half-subdued feelings of guilt, seeing him before consummation as confident, gay and pressing, a 'Merry Merry Sparrow' going 'swift as arrow' to his object; and after consummation as a creature subdued, but endeared to her – the 'Pretty Pretty Robin' who sobs. Nothing takes place in darkness or secrecy here, lovers are to be admired, and the embrace takes place beneath the green leaves of daylight, the open air, spring and summer, warmth and freshness.

An unsullied simplicity of delight in the sexual act, as exemplified in *The Blossom*, is probably not found very often. For most persons, the sexual aspect of life has been made, to some degree, complicated and mysterious by the time they reach maturity, and their thoughts about the matter are more likely to resemble those found in *The Sick Rose* than those of the innocent poem. It does not seem likely that Blake presents the two songs in order that we should simply admire the purity of the innocent attitude and deplore the aberrations of experience, however. The matter is more complex than that. The attitude of the Blossom is a little too simple, she approaches sexual activity in very much the same way as she might approach more trivial activities, and the degree of ease and purity shown seems too good to be altogether true. Something of a storm if not necessarily a 'howling storm' seems more natural to human beings; *The Sick Rose* carries us more deeply into the soul, and the elements we find there are not only those that we have so far indicated – there are positive as well as negative aspects to be found, healthy attractions as well as revulsions. The worm may be like a beast of prey but he is vigorous and powerful in his flight through the storm, and storms may terrify, but be overwhelming and thrilling. The Rose is associated with sickness but is also described as a 'bed of crimson joy', associating her with a luxury of abandonment which is, yet, vividly intense. The embrace of the last two lines is destructive, but fierce and ardent in its dark secrecy. The complexities of *The Sick Rose* bring in a rich eroticism which the innocent poem does not take into account, and the experienced speaker cannot help expressing the beauty of his theme, despite his apparent aversion.

2

IMAGINATIVE AND DOGMATIC THOUGHT

'Innocence' is a term which we apply, usually, to animals, to children, and to adults who lead an uncomplicated existence. Creatures who are limited in any way by their capacities or range of possible activities find it easier to come to terms with their world and with themselves – their behaviour is more spontaneous and they find their fulfilment easily. More developed creatures have a more difficult task and their failures are frequent. As our experience increases, it is more difficult to behave spontaneously because we must make complicated choices, and as our minds and tastes are cultivated so we become more artificial in our behaviour and enjoyments. Children have a natural grace which asserts itself easily, but which is rarely seen in the sophisticated adult except in persons with a great natural sweetness of mind. Innocent moments are of greater value in the adult – they bring a more complex being and a wider knowledge into balance than in the case of the child – but such moments are infrequent because of the difficulty experienced by a mature person in coming to terms with a complicated world. There is always the temptation, in Experience, to ignore the world in which one lives because then one may make decisions more easily. The child shows an interest in the minute details of objects. He wonders at things and is fascintaed by them. The cultivated adult, on the other hand, fails to observe much of what goes on about him, subordinates his activities to his interests, has little left to wonder at, and is too confident of his knowledge of things to find them fascinating. It is only rarely that the adult is held spell-bound in the manner of the speaker in *The Tyger*. We are normally too preoccupied, too prejudiced, too self-centred or too dogmatic to do justice to the possibilities of the world about us, and prefer to ignore or distort it. We lack fulfilment because we are interested in fulfilling only ourselves. Blake contrasts the self-centred greed of the state of Experience with the possibilities of our innocent moments in a fragment written in his *Notebook* called *Eternity*:

> He who bends to himself a joy
> Does the winged life destroy;
> But he who kisses the joy as it flies
> Lives in Eternity's sun rise.

The person described in the first two lines is too grasping to be able to gain what he might possess. He is selfishly determined to have an experience utterly and to retain it permanently, with the result that it becomes an encumbrance. The word 'bends' implies that the joy is forced to the will of the possessor but also that the joy is tied to him so as to restrict him, or that he is so engaged in holding the joy in an unnatural position that he cannot move as he should, while the joy is denied its flexibility and lightness. Joy is, by nature, a 'winged', swift, elusive and vital experience that can be contacted in a brief 'kiss' by swift, perceptive persons capable of letting it go when its time is past. The itch to possess or keep it nullifies it, though it can, paradoxically, be appreciated by those who are not anxious in their attempts to gain it. Those who truly know joy live in 'Eternity's sun rise', not because the pleasure may be indefinitely prolonged – joy is winged and flies away – but because the enjoyer is relaxed in his sense of gain, has no thoughts about the duration of the experience and so knows its full promise – the freshness and new creation of its 'sun rise'. He is fully aware of his world which may dawn and be fulfilled, whereas his rapacious counterpart destroys what he clutches at.

Selfishness, anxiety, insensitivity and meddlesomeness are characteristic of the experienced state, and they all militate against a generous appreciation of the events of life. We assert our own interests in a way which does not allow us to appreciate the happenings of the world, and so are left with nothing significant towards which our interest may be directed. Nearly all the *Songs of Experience* depict persons who have, without knowing it, defended themselves from the experience of things in some way or other. They are assertive persons who suppose that they are wise, but their assertive wisdom is what prevents them from seeing very much, and in his illustrations Blake often depicts experienced man as a greybeard who has lost the use of his senses. Sometimes he is lame as well. There are many insidious ways in which we deny ourselves a full life, and reading Blake's poems often brings home to us with a shock the knowledge of our own ways of crippling ourselves, though this knowledge is accompanied, unfortunately, by the realization that there is very little we can do to alter our condition. One of our most common ways of denying the world is represented in *Ah! Sun-flower*, one of the *Songs of Experience*:

AH! SUN-FLOWER

Ah Sun-flower! weary of time.
Who countest the steps of the Sun:
Seeking after that sweet golden clime
Where the travellers journey is done

Where the Youth pined away with desire.
And the pale Virgin shrouded in snow:
Arise from their graves and aspire.
Where my Sun-flower wishes to go.

Blake apparently feels pity for his flower, for he opens the poem with a sigh and he addresses it endearingly as 'my Sun-flower' in the last line. However, his pity is accompanied by the smile that signifies a touch of amusement if not of slight condescension. The Sun-flower, like the Youth and the Virgin, is pathetic, but this is because of its mistaken attitude, not because of any ill fortune. It does not appear to do much with its life except long for a destination which it will never reach. It gazes at higher things all day, but its 'travelling' is limited to desiring to arrive, for flowers must stay rooted in one spot if they are to remain alive. The Youth and the Virgin are in a similar condition, for they, too, long for the 'sweet golden clime' where there will be no more to wish for. They 'aspire', longing like the heliotropic Sun-flower, for things above them, and the Youth is 'pined away with desire', though the desire is for things as nebulous as the sighs he utters. He wastes away in his longing, but it is the act of desiring that wastes him, not deprivation of a particular thing – if he is deprived it is because he is so intent on wishing for what is above or beyond him that he does not accept the benefits he could have. Specifically, the aspirations of Youth and Virgin might be for the heaven to be gained in an after-life, when they have arisen from their graves, and reached the soul's ultimate destination. Perhaps that is why they deny themselves in this life, allowing their thoughts of what is to come to make them discontented with that whey have, and repressing the desires that this life thrusts upon us for the sake of what they hope to get in eternity. This renunciation of the world, however, is not a positive one, undertaken in the hope of gaining spiritual insight, but a negative rejection of what this life has to offer, undertaken in the hope of a reward after death. The notion is impious, for it treats the gift of life with ingratitude, and the Virgin is described as 'shrouded' in her cold and pointless chastity because her life, like the Youth's, is a 'grave' of mistaken self-denial.

Misconceived aspirations may waste our energies and render our lives sterile. Blake's poem, however, refers to more insidious influences than the conscious longings we may attribute to the Youth and Virgin. The Sun-flower's desires are for a rather indefinite state of hoped-for fulfilment, known to be 'sweet' and 'golden', but not formulated in precise terms, and it is 'wearied' by the endless travelling that keeps it in the same spot. To match this discontent, the poem, which is cast as a single sentence, has no main verb so that the reader is left unfulfilled and uneasy, and this adds to the suspicion that the Sun-flower will never find its blissful 'clime'. Experienced man spends much of his time in a state of discontent, hoping for something other than what he has got, always looking forward to some more blessed condition, though when he achieves it he finds it is something else he wants after all. Perhaps this drives us forward through our lives, but it also ensures that we can never relax sufficiently to enjoy what we have; we are incapable of 'kissing the joy as it flies', and always looking forward to some future time as we count the wearisome 'steps' of our present attainment. Often, we do not even formulate some specific goal, but negatively aspire to have done with what we are doing. During a large part of our lives the present is a burden that remains ever with us, and our life becomes a 'grave' which is 'pined away' for some attainment ever in the future, or for a state of existence which we never clearly conceive.

The Sun-flower succumbs to the temptation to set aside the real good of a lived life in the present for the delusive benefits of anti-cipation. Other temptations are equally subtle. We may, for instance, give in to the temptation of pursuing abstract notions of duty to the detriment of real affections and sympathies. In his *Holy Thursday* poems Blake shows how this may occur.

HOLY THURSDAY

Twas on a Holy Thursday their innocent faces clean
The children walking two & two in red & blue & green
Grey headed beadles walkd before with wands as white as snow
Till into the high dome of Pauls they like Thames waters flow

O what a multitude they seemd these flowers of London town
Seated in companies they sit with radiance all their own
The hum of multitudes was there but multitudes of lambs
Thousands of little boys & girls raising their innocent hands

Now like a mighty wind they raise to heaven the voice of song
Or like harmonious thunderings the seats of heaven among
Beneath them sit the aged men wise guardians of the poor
Then cherish pity; lest you drive an angel from your door

HOLY THURSDAY

Is this a holy thing to see.
In a rich and fruitful land
Babes reduced to misery
Fed with cold and usurous hand?

Is that trembling cry a song?
Can it be a song of joy?
And so many children poor?
It is a land of poverty!

And their sun does never shine.
And their fields are bleak & bare.
And their ways are fill'd with thorns
It is eternal winter there.

For where-e'er the sun does shine.
And where-e'er the rain does fall:
Babe can never hunger there,
Nor poverty the mind appall.

The poems describe a service in St. Paul's Cathedral attended by the charity school children of London. Some thousands of these children were brought to the Cathedral on special occasions and were seated together, each school wearing its own uniform dress. The sight must have been one to excite feeling, though very different feelings are aroused in the speakers of the two poems. Charity boys and girls were children who would have been left destitute had it not been for the existence of the schools, instituted privately by the wealthier citizens of London. The benefactors would give various reasons for maintaining the schools. These motives were usually of a religious or humanitarian nature, but it was often thought necessary to justify the institutions as a good investment for the community. The children, it was argued, were prevented from becoming criminals, they were given religious instruction, and the degree of literacy attained was sufficient to make them useful as servants without allowing them to compete with their betters. The 'wise guardians' of charity schools were often obliged to defend their enterprises against attack by putting forward such arguments of expediency, and making it publicly known that their charity was given grudgingly and as an investment.

The speaker of the experienced poem assumes, not perhaps without reason, that charity is based on selfish considerations. His indictment goes further than this, however. It horrifies him to think that charity, in any form and from any motive, should be necessary, and its existence indicates a failure on man's part to order his affairs properly. Men keep religious festivals and attend

religious services, but these facile observances conceal a fundamental indifference. No man really loves his fellows, and where
charity is to be found, it is given in self-defence. Men are pious
hypocrites who observe only those holy duties which it profits
them to keep; the service in St. Paul's is a mockery, and in the
first line of the poem the speaker challenges its validity. The
sacred duty of the Christian is to love his neighbour, and in a
society where this duty was observed social evils, which thrive on
indifference, could not exist. Behind the façade of holy observance, behind a make-believe of love of God and love of one's
neighbour, there are concealed the real conditions of social
existence – self-interest and the fear which allow a little charity to
be given with a 'cold and usurous hand'. All is pretence in such a
society. The hymn of praise and joy sung by the children is a
'trembling cry' – a precarious and uncertain wailing, indicative
of the real insecurity. The magnificence of the occasion is an
empty parade, and the prosperity it seems to indicate is false.
Though England appears to be a 'rich and fruitful land' this can
only be a sham if poor people exist. The speaker knows that the
fields of England are not 'bleak and bare', that the sun does shine
and the rain does fall; there is enough to supply everybody, but
indignation and horror at the evidence of poverty now presented
causes him to challenge the apparent prosperity, and claim that it
is a fiction. The reality is a condition of 'Babes reduced to misery',
of civil bankruptcy so that the public ways are 'fill'd with thorns',
and of an unproductive 'eternal winter'.

The observer in the experienced poem takes the sceptic's view
of the proceedings in St. Paul's, and would dismiss the innocent
poem as superficial and sentimental. The innocent speaker is certainly taken up by the religious service (or is 'taken in', his experienced counterpart would say), and submits his feelings to the
scene. The first stanza emphasizes the order and decorum of the
occasion. The procession is regular, the children uniform in dress
as well as in their formation, but they are brightly regular in their
different colours with a simple dignity which is complemented by
the more stately gravity of the beadles. The steady pace of the procession, the underlying stability it represents and the grandeur of

so orderly a movement taking place beneath the imposing dome are all brought out by the comparison with the even stateliness of flow of the river Thames.

In the second and third stanzas the ideas of multitude and order, simple innocence and dignity are combined with references to the hosts of heaven. The children show the delicacy of 'flowers', their cleanliness and youthfulness are seen as a 'radiance' and they 'raise their hands' in gestures that show helplessness combined with grace of movement and a splendid beauty. Like the hosts who praise God, the children are seated in companies. They are similar to those who (in Revelation 14) 'are without fault before the throne of God':

And I looked, and lo, a Lamb stood on the mount Sion, and with him an hundred forty and four thousand . . . And I heard a voice from heaven as the voice of many waters, and as the voice of a great thunder . . . And they sung as it were a new song before the throne. . . . These are they which follow the Lamb whithersoever he goeth. These were redeemed from among men, being the first-fruits unto God and to the Lamb.

There are echoes, in the song, of this passage, of other passages from the Bible and of accounts of heaven found in the traditional mythology of Christianity. Blake does not quote exactly or with due regard to context – he seldom does – but he reminds us of various descriptions of heaven, and reminds us also that when the disciples asked, 'Who is the greatest in the Kingdom of heaven?' – Christ set a child in their midst, saying, 'who so shall receive one such little child in my name receiveth me' (Matthew 18. 5).

There is a proper place in this ordered multitude, so reminiscent of the celestial choirs, for the 'wise guardians of the poor' – those who have received little children in Christ's name by founding and maintaining the schools. They are those who 'cherish pity', and they are seen as benevolent and disinterested men who have ordered things well, who are worthy of respect and act as an example to others. Their presence reminds the speaker that we receive the divine presence in relieving our fellows, or, in St. Paul's words, we should not be 'forgetful to entertain strangers: for thereby some have entertained angels unawares'.

In the *Holy Thursday* poems Blake presents two views of the service in St Paul's which are so different that they challenge us to decide which is the right one. In one sense of the word, each poem is 'right' for the frame of mind of the person who speaks the poem. They see different things. But we may still ask which observer sees to better purpose, and the answer seems to be that, despite the greater worldly wisdom, and despite the apparently superior moral interest shown in the experienced poem, it is the innocent song that displays greater insight and a more responsible attitude. We cannot look on the poem as being an ironical exposé of the sentimental view when we see that the speaker takes more into account and is less one-sided in his approach than his experienced counterpart. The innocent speaker sees more of the scene than the experienced one. There is a wealth of detail given in the poem – details of the dress and disposition of the various persons, their gestures, and the sounds they make. The detail is interpreted as it is given, but it is there, while the experienced poem contains hardly any detail at all. We know what occasion the experienced poem describes only because the title tells us, we must fill in the sequence of incidents from our own knowledge, and all we are told of the event is that a song is being sung, presumably by the children who are spoken of as poor. The speaker offers no other observations whatever and the rest of the poem is taken up with his opinion of the scene he refrains from describing. The reader gains the impression that the experienced speaker is incapable of seeing very much because his interpretation crowds eagerly in, obscuring his vision. He is so forward in asserting his moral ideas that the scene in St Paul's becomes an excuse for a sermon rather than a circumstance he can give attention to. This impression is heightened when we examine the nature of his moral preoccupation and compare it with the sense of responsibility felt in the innocent song.

The experienced song conveys a strong feeling and conveys it

powerfully but the feeling is not, in itself, subtle or likely to persist for long. The horror felt by the speaker amounts almost to a
fascination. He certainly does not *think* about poverty in any sense
of the word that involves an orderly development of ideas. There
is only one idea – that no land can be termed wealthy where
poverty is possible – and that idea, with the indignant misery felt
by the speaker, is repeated over and over again in the first two and
last ten lines of the poem. The speaker describes poverty as a fact
that 'appalls' the mind. Dismay paralyses his thought. He is
rendered helpless to do anything except feel the dreadfulness of
the situation and the misery of his own despair. There is no hint
in the poem that he feels that there is anything he can do to help
matters. The evil is a social one and flourishes on too wide a scale
for him to feel anything but overcome and helpless, and in time,
as no further thought or action seems likely to develop, the feeling
will pass away. Feelings of indignation or despair about social or
cosmic injustices usually occur fitfully, while a quieter sympathy,
accompanied by more positive acts of pity, may persist in a steadier
manner.

The social indictment in the experienced poem is accompanied
by strong feelings, but the impression that they are phrenetic is
reinforced by the fact that they have a dogmatic basis. The speaker
is prepared to account for the motives of all men according to a
formula. The children are the recipients of charity, and where
charity is seen it is to be accounted for in terms of a calculated
self-interest which is 'cold' and 'usurous'. No doubt this may
often be the case, but the speaker asserts that it is always so. The
low view of humanity – the view that our real motives are always
selfish, whether we care to pretend to being altruistic or not – is
the easy view to take. But this cheapening of human motives and
their reduction to a sordid principle is similar to the opposite
insistence on always taking the elevated view, in that both betoken
inelasticity and immaturity of thought. The experienced speaker
feels strongly but is not really exercising his mind. It is true that
he might seem to be an enlightened thinker because he apparently
penetrates to the real significance of the service in St. Paul's. But
his present thoughts are not the outcome of the present occasion.

The sight of the children is no more than an excuse for a habit of feeling and an established pattern of ideas to reassert themselves in a form modified to suit the moment. The children are not seen or cared for except as they provide an opportunity for the generalization that is produced.

The innocent speaker shows fascination of a different sort. He is impressed by what he sees and is carried away by the spectacle. Perhaps it is naïve to be so easily impressed, but the speaker is capable of giving attention, and if the experienced poem demonstrates an extreme of 'realism', it cannot be said that the innocent one shows the opposite extreme of sentimentality. The speaker does not undertake to explain the social conditions that give rise to the spectacle, nor does he attempt to account for the motives of the 'wise guardians'. Poverty is taken merely as something that exists and because it exists any attempt to alleviate it is regarded as well directed. The emotion felt by the speaker may be impulsive, even uncritical, but it is, at least, an immediate reaction to a real circumstance and not a stereotyped response that blots out the circumstance almost entirely.

Morally, the innocent speaker shows a more responsible attitude. The experienced speaker is left without any duty. The evil is too basic – is built into the fabric of society – and those who do find a duty to perform merely add their quota of evil. For the innocent speaker there is a duty: 'Then cherish pity; lest you drive an angel from your door.' The moral is stated artlessly, but is not as uncomplicated as might appear at first sight. Just as the service in St Paul's is related to nothing beyond itself, so charity towards others is related to nothing beyond the deed performed. Pity is to be shown for its own sake. No idea of reward, either now or hereafter, is implied. One must show pity merely because not doing so might deny someone capable of receiving it. Angels are entertained unawares and they are turned away unawares, so any satisfaction to be gained is merely the satisfaction of a charitable impulse, and who could fail to exercise that desire? The innocent song ends on a positive note without preaching a sermon, while the experienced speaker preaches a sermon that is negative in tone, being full of moral anxiety but destructive of moral obligation.

Our thinking is not a mechanical process which, computer-like, involves the manipulation of precise observations in order to reach an inevitable result. The conclusions reached by the innocent and experienced speakers of the *Holy Thursday* poems are different and the observations they make are different too. The experienced speaker inhibits his senses in order to assert an abstruse notion, while the charitable mind of the innocent speaker allows him to take a keen interest in the doings of other persons. No doubt there is much to admire in the experienced speaker. He feels strongly, he has a conscience and he is earnestly outspoken. In his own way he has a feeling of involvement and his concern is a serious one. The sort of thinking he displays is unavoidable in Experience, but comparison with the innocent mode shows that it is basically irresponsible because it is out of touch with real persons, with present events and with personal duties. There is no help for this state of affairs. To pretend an interest that is not really felt would be hypocritical, and the experienced mind is most profitably engaged in pondering its speculative problems in the hope that it will arrive, speculatively, at a solution, with some practical benefits. The innocent mind sees no problem, not because it is foolish, but because spontaneous feelings of charity direct its thought into a more immediately relevant channel.

Blake contrasts the innocent grasp on immediate reality against experienced withdrawal in many of the songs. Anxious desires render the Sun-flower incapable of living. An anguished sense of social injustice dominates the awareness of the experienced speaker in *Holy Thursday*, and the same sense of injustice is shown by the experienced chimney sweeper in his song. The innocent sweeper, by contrast, shows that he has a freer intelligence and a fine sense of duty.

The Chimney Sweeper

A little black thing among the snow:
Crying weep, weep, in notes of woe!
Where are thy father & mother? say?
They are both gone up to the church to pray.

Because I was happy upon the heath.
And smil'd among the winters snow:
They clothed me in the clothes of death.
And taught me to sing the notes of woe.

And because I am happy. & dance & sing.
They think they have done me no injury:
And are gone to praise God & his Priest & King
Who make up a heaven of our misery.

The Chimney Sweeper

When my mother died I was very young.
And my father sold me while yet my tongue,
Could scarcely cry weep weep weep weep.
So your chimneys I sweep & in soot I sleep.

Theres little Tom Dacre who cried when his head
That curl'd like a lambs back, was shav'd, so I said.
Hush Tom never mind it, for when your head's bare.
You know that the soot cannot spoil your white hair.

And so he was quiet, & that very night,
As Tom was a sleeping he had such a sight,
That thousands of sweepers Dick, Joe Ned & Jack
Were all of them lock'd up in coffins of black

And by came an Angel who had a bright key,
And he open'd the coffins & set them all free.
Then down a green plain leaping laughing they run
And wash in a river and shine in the Sun.

Then, naked & white, all their bags left behind.
They rise upon clouds, and sport in the wind.
And the Angel told Tom if he'd be a good boy,
He'd have God for his father & never want joy.

And so Tom awoke and we rose in the dark
And got with our bags & our brushes to work.
Tho' the morning was cold, Tom was happy & warm
So if all do their duty, they need not fear harm.

Dickens has vividly described some of the unfortunate human beings to be seen on the streets of London a century ago, and in Blake's day, half a century before that, conditions were even worse. Of all states of wretchedness to be encountered, that of the chimney-sweeper was, perhaps, the most miserable and the most capable of moving the Londoner's heart to pity. These children were apprenticed when they were hardly more than infants because at that age their size allowed them to enter the flues. Long before the fires of the day were lit they were at work inside chimneys that were probably hot from the day before, their masters were notoriously brutal, and if they escaped death by falling or suffocation, they were carried off at an early age by malnutrition, ill-treatment, and the various ailments brought on by soot and the stifling conditions of their labour. These children were the objects of pity, and attempts were made to alleviate their lot by recommending laws to regulate their conditions of employment, but the evil, like most social evils, resisted attempts to legislate it away. The reformer always alarms his fellow citizens because his proposed reforms seem to endanger the present structure of society, and it is only after a long struggle that improved laws are accepted, often only after the evil has taken a new and unforeseen form. In *London*, Blake writes:

How the Chimney-sweepers cry
Every blackning Church appalls.

The Church is not indifferent to the miseries of the sweeper – quite the contrary, it is horrified, but it is apparently helpless to remove the evil or to get to the root of poverty and ill-treatment. The Christian ideal of the brotherhood of man seems no closer to fulfilment after centuries of effort than at the beginning of our era, and the Church, like all institutions, seems too ponderous to keep pace with the twists and evasions of its enemy. The word 'appalls' implies that though the Church may feel shock and anguish at man's inhumanity, it can only stand by, inarticulate, faint and helpless. More cynically, the word may imply that a pall of corruption has crept over the Church, just as a black pall of soot has crept over the façade of the Church building – an outward sign of spiritual indifference, as the chimney-sweeper, also covered in soot, is a sign of society's callous acceptance of suffering crying in its midst.

Cynicism is carried further in the experienced sweeper's song, where, in the last two lines, the Church and the state are seen as being in league to maintain an unjust order of things. In the society implied in that poem it is the hypocrite and the self-deceiver who flourish at the expense of the unfortunate, and they maintain their comfort by establishing themselves respectably in a system that is designed to favour the determined self-seeker. The Church may say fine-sounding things about a divine order, and may declare that civil order is linked to it, with the king acting as God's regent on earth, but to the chimney-sweeper who enjoys none of the benefits of the world it seems, not surprisingly, as if this grand design is a convenient fiction, subscribed to by the more fortunate inhabitants of the earth, who 'make up a heaven of his misery'. The word 'heaven' is well chosen, implying a sanctuary for the self-satisfaction and insensitivity of those who have established themselves comfortably. They are of the elect, inhabit a world within the world where they feel insulated, and are smugly unaware of the plight of less fortunate mortals whom they intentionally or unintentionally exploit. They have domesticated God in this heaven as the servant of state, Church and self-interest, and 'gone up to the Church' like the Pharisee who 'went up to the temple to pray' (Luke 18), assured of his own rectitude.

The parents are hypocritically self-righteous and determined to enjoy the best of all worlds. Their devotions are paid to gain a selfish comfort of mind in their present 'heaven' as well as to ensure that they will be received in any heaven yet to come, and there are other ways of smothering any feeling of guilt they might have. Anyone who has lived in a society where there is a wide gap between the rich and poor knows that it is among the poor that any open expression of gaiety is to be found, and that the wealthy are very much in the habit of pointing this out to each other as a justification for maintaining the state of things as it exists. The sweeper's parents, observing the natural exuberance of their child when it breaks out in dancing and singing, may feel that, after all, he is not so badly off, and so suppress any thought that they may have done him 'injury' in selling him into 'apprenticeship'. In such ways they have soothed their feelings, and their child has sufficient insight to have detected their hypocrisy. His insight goes further, and in stanza two he imputes to his parents motives of jealousy and ill-will. Consciously or unconsciously, they resented his spontaneous childish happiness, so alien to the austere and grasping satisfactions of their own lives, and deliberately or instinctively they sought to kill his spirit by putting him into the black 'clothes' of the sweep and by sending him to 'sing' the tradesman's cry of the sweeper in the streets – a cry that sounds like the lament of the boy for his own 'woe'.

The experienced sweeper's song indicts the boy's parents and is an indictment of the social order in which they have established a position, even though that position is a humble one. The poem goes further, for the boy suggests in the last two lines that the universe has thrust him out, and those like him – that is how it seems to one placed as he is. In the innocent song, too, there is an indictment, but it is a limited one and it is made in a different manner. Perhaps the sweep's mother may have protected him, but after her death his father has been callous enough to 'sell' him for the pitiful sum usually offered. A wretched story of poverty, and all its attendant ills may be imagined, but the poem does not lead our thoughts to wider social issues. The accusation, if it is an accusation, is specifically directed to the person responsible for the sweeper's plight and it refers to the father's act without attempting to explain the mental processes that gave rise to it. The experienced poem is much concerned with explaining things – the motives of the parents and the position of the sweep in the order of things – and the poem uses words appropriate to its explanatory nautre: 'Because', 'And because'. The innocent poem recounts events and is expressed in the language of narrative: 'When', 'And', 'So', 'so', 'And so', 'And', 'And', 'Then', 'And', 'And so', 'So'. The little boy merely tells us what he has first-hand knowledge of, and he tells us without attempting to direct our interpretation. Blake's use of rhythm is very subtle. The experienced poem is written with a regular beat. It slips glibly off the tongue, for the speaker is ready with an explanation of things. The first stanza of the innocent song has a different rhythm. If Blake had wished to impose a regular metre on the poem, he might have written the first line as, 'My mother died when I was very young', but the word order he chose to use has the effect of throwing the emphasis on 'When'. The child is not laying stress on his woeful condition or asking for pity, but indicating one of the events that have led to his present circumstances. He is being factual, the first line is in the rhythm of explanatory prose, and the remainder of the stanza follows in the same manner. The boy deserves pity – Blake makes that quite clear – but he is not asking for it, and the tone he adopts has the dignity of unselfconscious, patient narrative. As in the case of the experienced poem, someone has asked him to explain his position, but this sweep does so briefly and frankly, allowing the facts to speak for themselves, and he does so without complaining. He knows quite well that his circumstances are wretched, and briefly describes them in the fourth line, but accepts them without being passively submissive or resentful. 'That is the way I must live', he seems to say and he accepts his way of life with the fortitude expressed in the last line of the poem.

The experienced sweeper speaks in a shrewder vein. The first three lines of his poem belong to the person who interrogates him, and the remaining line of the stanza, which begins his reply, is, because of its isolation, very abrupt. The boy is quick to give his answer with its implied accusation that the parents are pious hypocrites, and he is quick with his explanation of the motives that allow them to view his plight with indifference. He is ready, also, with his disillusioned statement on social injustice. The child is in a wretched condition, but he is rather glib and very worldly-wise for his age, so that it is difficult to admire him. Those who deserve our pity do not necessarily command our respect, and the child's aggrieved and self-centred tone makes him unpleasant. He is sufficiently 'knowing', even, to be able to remark on his own apparent happiness – on his ability to dance and sing – in the course of his explanation. The explanation itself shows a certain amount of cynical insight into the mentality of those who are determined to cling to what they possess, but it takes a limited view of Church and state and has something of the formula about it. The early seventeen-nineties was a period during which revolutionary truisms were much bandied about, and sentiments similar to those in the poem may be found in the popular writings of Tom Paine or Mary Wollstonecraft. The sweeper shows no unexpected insight into his position, nor does he lay bare to us the truth of his situation without consciously meaning to. He merely applies psychological and political theories to his description of himself and his parents – theories which are stereotyped and only partially true.

The innocent chimney sweeper shows real insight, he does so without attempting to theorize, and does so, oddly enough, by bringing certain stereotyped phrases to life. The last line of the poem, for instance, if taken in isolation, sounds like the repetition of a very trite and unpleasant sentiment: 'So if all do their duty, they need not fear harm.' This is the sort of thing that is said, in one form or another, in order to keep people submissive, especially people to whom harm has come in good measure. The sweep has probably been told very often that we must perform our tasks in that state to which it has pleased God to call us and that we should be obedient to those set in authority over us. He accepts this notion, but he does not accept it in a supine spirit. On the contrary, he applies it very vigorously, not only to the sweeping of chimneys, which was probably what it was meant to be applied to when he heard it, but also to the support he can give others. In the course of the poem we have seen him doing his duty to little Tom, and we have seen the loving spirit in which he has performed it, so that when we come to read the last line we see that duty has a real meaning here, and that though harm has come to the sweep he has something to offset it: the fact that he is responsively alive in his situation and not, like the experienced sweep, or his parents, stifled by considerations that are merely selfish. The innocent sweep does not suggest that if one does one's duty, no harm will come to one. He is far too much of the realist to think that. But he does say that when harm comes one may stand up to it. He can stand up to

it because, instead of accepting his fortune in the miserable isolation of accusation and self-pity, he finds that it presents him with
an opportunity to be active and useful. In his month the last line
of the poem is not an unpleasant commonplace, but an exact and
unassuming statement of the manner in which he meets his
situation.

The words of consolation spoken to little Tom Dacre in the
second stanza are also, taken out of context, stereotyped and unpleasant, but taken in the setting of the poem are comforting and
brave. These words must have been heard often enough by those
whose heads had been cropped. Unimaginative persons probably
tried to console sweepers in this way, though as the consolation
overlooks the fact that the hair has been lost, it was probably
designed to quieten the social conscience of the speaker rather
than to add to the real comfort of the suffer. The sweeper who
speaks the words is not unimaginative because, as his plight is
the same as little Tom's, and as he is facing a situation with little
Tom, he speaks a whole truth and not a partial one. An outsider,
making such a statement, would be leaving out of account what
he should not ignore: the injustice of the loss of the hair, while
the chimney sweeper, being a fellow-sufferer, can make the
remark as a statement of fact without being appalled by the
injustice. If an outsider made the statement he would show himself insensitive or unkind, but the sweeper can make the same
statement to show understanding of the sweeper's situation and to
convey sympathy to his little companion. It is the fellow-feeling
that only he can give which quietens little Tom.

The chimney-sweeper uses statements which are trite, but
breathes new life into them. The innocent imagination does not
strain after novelty, but is, nevertheless, always fresh, and this is
true of little Tom's dream which is composed of very unoriginal
material, made beautiful in the poem. Angels, risen souls upon
clouds, an existence in another world that 'never wants joy', the
fatherly figure of God, are all stereotypes of Sunday-school
instruction, though they come as fresh thoughts to children
and are accepted with wonder and pleasure. Blake's description
is very fresh; he conveys the wonder of the child, so that it is only

after reflection that the dream is seen as made up of commonplace ideas. The contrasts made are striking and vivid. 'Coffins of black' refer us not only to the death of the sweepers, but also to their deathly lives, imprisoned in chimneys and 'locked up' in poverty and ill-usage; and this state is contrasted with the excited freedom of movement taking place in the open 'green plain' where the sweepers run 'leaping' and 'laughing' – joyous acts leading to the complete release as the boys, now 'naked' and unencumbered, 'rise upon clouds, and sport in the wind'. Once out of the coffins, the sweepers are taken to a brilliant world – the Angel's key is 'bright', and the boys, washed and refreshed in the river, now 'shine in the sun' and are 'white'.

Some well-meaning adult must have told Tom of a heaven where God and his angels make all things well, a notion which can be unpleasant and irreverent if used to make men passive in their attitude towards the present world. Tom's notion is not passive. The Angel does, it is true, liberate him from the black coffin of his deathly existence so that he may be active and joyful in heaven in the manner now denied him, and he is to have a loving Father after death if he behaves well now, but it is not merely because he feels that he is to be recompensed that the dream makes Tom 'happy and warm'. He has the dream as a consequence of being comforted by the older boy, and if he can think of the love God will give him later it is because he has received the affection of his friend now. His idea of a place where all shall be loved is given support by the fact that he has known the warmth of the fellow-feeling his companion can give. It is significant that he has the dream after the gesture made by the older sweeper has given a meaning to the Sunday-school myth, and his statement of the myth is an affirmation of the existence of love, not a selfish wish for compensation.

The state of Innocence is not a condition of ignorance or of naïveté, even though children and folk who lead a simple life are most usually associated with the state. Little Tom does not know much, he very readily believes what he is told, and we may call him innocent, but his older companion is equally innocent, though he knowns a great deal and is certainly not gullible. Tom believes his Sunday-school story of the Angel, and turns it to good purpose, while the older boy sees the good purpose without either believing or disbelieving the story. For him, it would be irrelevant to consider the verity of a belief which affirms the efficacy of human sympathy, for if God means anything at all he means it to those who have affections to be touched. The chimney-sweeper is wise, while the parents of the experienced sweeper who have 'gone up to the church to pray' are naïve, for they suppose that God will conduct a business transaction with them. The innocent sweeper does not bother to explain events, not because he is incapable of doing so, but because he is engaged in meeting them positively and vigorously. There is not much cheer in his life, as he knows very well indeed, but he turns what he can into a joy to be kissed 'as it flies'. No joy is more 'eternal' than the affection which he unpretentiously shows. The materials he has to work with – the truisms he offers for comfort – are dilapidated, and should be ugly. He makes them firm and beautiful, infusing them with his generous spirit, We see the same generosity in the speaker of the innocent *Holy Thursday* where the simple moral – hardly a moral at all – is quite unselfish, and the description of the scene shows a mind free to observe and be sympathetic. The thoughts of the experienced sweeper and of the observer in the experienced *Holy Thursday* are more complex, though neither speaker shows any originality, and their words are not very profound. However complex, their thoughts are less valuable because there is less life in them. They are not infused with generosity and they have an inert quality because they are generalized truths produced by the thinker for application to the situation in which he finds himself, and not a lively outcome of the circumstance itself. Thought may be a joy when it is alive and on the wing, but in Experience the thinker 'bends' the joy to himself, destroys thought in favour of rigidly held notions, becomes dogmatic, and allows even the most valuable ideas to become prejudices which limit his contact with his world instead of opening new approaches to it. Blake emphasizes this in many of the songs – in the two poems entitled *Nurse's Song*, for instance, the one innocent and the other experienced.

Nurse's Song

When the voices of children are heard on the green
And laughing is heard on the hill,
My heart is at rest within my breast
And everything else is still

Then come home my children the sun is gone down
And the dews of night arise
Come come leave off play, and let us away
Till the morning appears in the skies

No no let us play, for it is yet day
And we cannot go to sleep
Besides in the sky, the little birds fly
And the hills are all coverd with sheep

Well well go & play till the light fades away
And then go home to bed
The little ones leaped & shouted & laugh'd
And all the hills ecchoed

NURSES Song

When the voices of children are heard on the green
And whisprings are in the dale:
The days of my youth rise fresh in my mind,
My face turns green and pale.

Then come home my children, the sun is gone down
And the dews of night arise
Your spring & your day, are wasted in play
And your winter and night in disguise.

It is significant that one of these poems should be in the form of
a dialogue, the other a monologue. The innocent nurse is in
touch with things, her senses are receptive and she is open to persuasion, while her experienced sister, who communicates with no
one, is self-engrossed and assertive. The innocent nurse responds
to the stillness of evening, submitting herself to the quiet time of

35

day in a relaxed peacefulness with her heart 'at rest', and when the children ask for more time to play she indulgently allows then to decide for themselves when they should 'go home to bed'. Blake's illustration to the innocent song shows this nurse sitting apart reading a book while a number of children play a game. The nurse in the illustration to the experienced poem takes her duties more anxiously. In the illustration, her two charges are directly under her care. A girl is engaged in some improving activity, while a boy is having his hair combed and arranged. Both illustration and poem show that the experienced nurse does her work very conscientiously – perhaps too conscientiously to allow her to be a good nurse, for her suspicions and misgivings must create an atmosphere disturbing to the simplicity of young children.

These two poems are more obviously paired by Blake than the other examples we have examined. Not only are the titles identical, but the opening line of the first stanza and the first two lines of the second stanza, in each case, are the same, although in the different settings the lines have a very different impact. This emphasizes not only the difference in response made by the nurses, but also the similarity of their situation. It is not necessary to assume that the two young women have had different histories, so that the one is inclined to look cheerfully on her world and adopt an easy-going manner towards her children, while the other has reason to be fearful and protective. It is possible that the two nurses have enjoyed very much the same sort of past experience, but that each expresses a different impulse on the present occasion, and it is even possible that Blake means us to see these different modes of response as different ways in which a single mind might express itself. The two nurses may be one nurse as she finds herself at two different times, or the two poems may express two modes of response which endeavour to assert themselves on a single occasion. We are all innocent and experienced by turns so that even the most self-centred person may have his moments of 'glad grace' (or the possibility is always there) and even the most ingenuous child becomes, at times, self-conscious and affected. We may all, on occasion, shed our anxious state to 'kiss the joy as it flies' unless we are very unfortunate indeed, and it is rare for any individual to be so fortunate as to preserve Wordsworth's 'poetic spirit of our human life' unabated, unsuppressed, and 'pre-eminent till death'.

Human beings have their own character, but a wide range of potentialities, which circumstances may elicit. The common lines in the two nurses' songs illustrate the fact that words have a similar flexibility. They are stable things with their own individuality, but they take their life and full meaning from the context in which they are uttered. The same phrases have a very different significance in the two poems. The 'voices of children' which are heard in the first line of the experienced song are indistinct and disturbing in association with the 'whisprings in the dale' of the second line. The nurse senses furtive, probably indecent, 'goings on', and sees things as obscure and unhealthy, so that the sun which goes down in the fifth line holds no promise of rising again – there is no renewal – and the 'dews of night' are not revivifying but dank and unwholesome. The sun goes down in the innocent poem, but only until 'morning appears in the skies' and the 'dews of night' are a benefit which renews earth for the day to follow. The 'voices of children' of the first line are associated with the unpremeditated carelessness of 'laughing' coming clearly from the 'hill', where it is open and public. Our attention is taken outwards and upwards and to movement and light throughout the poem; to the sky of the sun and the birds, to the hills 'covered with sheep', and to the play of the children. The last two lines of the poem present us with vigour, spontaneity, clear vision and distinct sounds in an open landscape:

> The little ones leaped & shouted & laugh'd
> And all the hills ecchoed.

The children of the experienced poem are mute, sounds are muffled, and the nurse's world is indistinct and threatening.

It is in character that the experienced nurse should refer to her 'mind' while her innocent sister talks of her 'heart'. The experienced nurse sees very little because she is too engrossed in her fears and revulsions, and she imposes the pattern of her thoughts on her senses. To her, life is, at best, an aimless wearing away, and at the worst an accumulation of painful mistakes. The memory of her own youthful indiscretions haunts her, making her ill with shame and mistrustful of her charges. Her protectiveness is a result of suspicion, not only of her children, but of all men, whose instincts, she assumes, are such that they must be governed and constantly watched. Like other experienced speakers she has a dogmatic view, expressed as a generalization in the last two lines:

> Your spring and your day, are wasted in play
> And your winter and night in disguise.

The innocent song finished with a clear look at the events of the moment and a pleased appreciation of the scene, but the experienced nurse, seeing the same things, refuses to take them in, turning her attention instead to the disenchanted recesses of her mind. Man never knows what is good, she says, because when young we have no sense of what is serious ('play' is a meaningless waste of time), and the knowledge that might come with age is excluded by a barrier set up against the world. We 'disguise' and distort ourselves so that we no longer know what we are or what we want, becoming hidden in a tangle of habits as we enter the 'winter and night' of an isolation made more complete by advancing years. There is, of course, truth in what she says – this is a tendency to which we are subject – but it is not the whole truth nor is it the only truth, though the nurse is convinced, at the moment, of the adequacy of what she says. All seasons, for her, lead to a dismal close. The sun goes down to rise no more, and 'winter and night' come, like age, to finish a day, or a year, or a life that was endured, but that never had any real joy or significance. When she looks back on her own life the nurse experiences the sick feeling of humiliation, shame and frustration – her 'face turns green and pale', and her own 'spring and day', like that of her children, is seen as an agony of growing up to a regretful maturity. The innocent nurse, by contrast, responds with her 'heart', not because she is more easily pleased or less intelligent than her counterpart, but because her mood is a spontaneous reaction to the calm time of day and the pleasant season of the year, her inward 'rest' and mental calm contributing to the 'stillness' about her. In the sense of the word 'intelligence' implying 'awareness' she shows more of the quality than her sister, for she is alive to circumstances and can communicate with her children. She is a responsive being, not one set in opposition to hostile circumstances. She assumes that the impulses of man are benign, that he is best left in freedom to test their effects, and her first request: 'Then come home', is modified to 'then go home', which leaves the decision to the children. She does not fuss them or fret herself, and probably gets a respect and responsiveness denied to the experienced nurse who can command only obedience. The innocent nurse utters no 'truths' because she exhibits, in herself, the 'truth' of a human being living adequately in full possession of her senses as an inhabitant of her world, not as an alien passenger through it. She could discourse more fully on her state, no doubt, but does not choose to do so, for enjoyment of the kind she experiences need not be grasped at verbally, and though Blake's poem contains an appreciation of her state of mind, the comment made is an implicit one.

3

THE FALL FROM INNOCENCE

Blake's comment on his innocent nurse is an implicit one and he allows his experienced nurse to make a statement that is explicit, but he does not mean us to view the voice of experience as more intelligent, more penetrating, or even as more articulate. The wish to be explicit – to explain one's mind to oneself – may result in a statement that is limited or one-sided, while a more spontaneous utterance, being less purposefully controlled, may display more of what is in one's mind, even though one may not have meant it to emerge and be only vaguely aware of what one has said. The innocent nurse has values superior to her counterpart's, she does not mean to explain them to us, but they are embodied in her poem, and we are aware of them even before we determine exactly what they are. In daily conversations we are sensitive to meanings half-concealed in the speech of other people. Poetry, which makes the fullest possible use of all the resources of language, also contains these meanings, apparently hidden until we set about finding them, but which we may already have responded to in a 'natural' way. Presumably the poet puts such meanings into the poem without necessarily determining to do so. They are 'naturally' there because the poem is an expression of the whole being of the poet, and he may realize fully what he has said only after he has said it. Blake implies that inspiration of this sort is characteristic of the *Songs of Innocence* in his *Introduction* to the series, where he describes how poetry is made by the piper and enjoyed by the child.

Introduction

Piping down the valleys wild
Piping songs of pleasant glee
On a cloud I saw a child.
And he laughing said to me.

Pipe a song about a Lamb:
So I piped with merry chear.
Piper pipe that song again –
So I piped, he wept to hear.

Drop thy pipe thy happy pipe
Sing thy songs of happy chear.
So I sung the same again
While he wept with joy to hear.

Piper sit thee down and write
In a book that all may read –
So he vanish'd from my sight
And I pluck'd a hollow reed.

And I made a rural pen,
And I stain'd the water clear,
And I wrote my happy songs,
Every child may joy to hear

The songs show that Blake had a fine intellect, capable not only of careful observation, but of speculative flights. His assessment of the potentialities of the human mind shows profundity, and he is a philosopher-poet of great originality, though he avoids the methods of the philosopher, and makes no use of many of the resources of the poet. He seldom makes an abstract statement as a philosopher would, and yet the persons and circumstances described in his poems have an abstract quality not usually found in poetry. The songs do not express the feelings and thoughts of the poet on some specific occasion, as lyrical poetry very often does, and the children, the shepherds, and the other figures depicted in his verses are types of humanity, not individual human beings. It is easy to read many of the songs individually in the way nursery rhymes are read – as rather unreal but sharply drawn sketches with an element of the charming or the grotesque, and it is only when the poems are read together that one becomes aware of the life and reality of the mind and purpose behind them. The poem we are discussing offers very conventional figures of innocence: a shepherd with his pipe and a child, in a 'wild' and 'rural' setting, and their song is, very fittingly, about a 'Lamb'. It may be read as a happy song that 'Every child may joy to hear' – as a simple description which might entertain readers artless enough to enjoy it unthinkingly, but in addition it contains an implicit explanation of the nature of Innocence and adds to that a description of one of the ways in which poetry achieves its end. The poem may be read at more than one level, and an understanding of its various levels is more easily achieved if it is compared with the *Introduction* to the *Songs of Experience* (the Bard's song) and if Blake's illustrations depicting the piper and the child in their 'valley wild' are examined opposite.

In the copies of *Songs of Innocence and of Experience* made up by Blake himself the two plates are placed as frontispiece to each of the two series, the first before the *Songs of Innocence* and the second before the *Songs of Experience*, and it is clearly the first which is meant to directly represent the poem we are discussing. The piper has dropped his pipe to his side and looks up at the child who passes over his head on his cloud. There are trees on each side, and a flock of sheep is grazing in the background. In the second illustration the same elements are used except that the piper no longer has his pipe and the child no longer has his cloud, being equipped with the wings of a cherub instead. In the *Introduction* the child on his cloud is a vivid presence, but an elusive one which vanishes from the sight of the piper without an explanation, and without the piper wanting one:

> Piper sit thee down and write
> In a book that all may read –
> So he vanish'd from my sight
> And I pluck'd a hollow reed.

The vanishing is very abrupt, but the piper takes this for granted and sets about finding the instruments for writing – appropriately 'rural' ones befitting a song of Innocence. He enjoys the presence of the child while he is with him, acceding 'with merry chear' to the requests made, enjoying the 'laughing' delight that

his songs elicit; but he has no desire to cling to the enjoyment, and when the child vanishes he takes up a new activity: that of writing down how much he liked being with him – for his first task is to compose the song we are reading. Both piper and child have the ability, mentioned in the fragment *Eternity* (p. 15), of being able to kiss 'the joy as it flies', and they come together with pleasure and part without regret. The child delights in the game of ordering the adult about and listens to the music with tears of joy, then, child-like, he turns his attention elsewhere when he has had enough. His emotions are described in simple terms as 'laughing', 'weeping', and 'weeping with joy', the last description signifying, not that the emotion is excessive, but that it is heartfelt, and not easily categorized. The piper enjoys making his music, enjoys seeing the pleasure he gives, and changes from one activity to another (from piping to singing to writing) with ease. As he is depicted in the 'innocent' illustration his ease and versatility are indicated, as well as his ability to give his full attention: his movement forward is arrested, but about to be carried on. He gazes full into the face of the child, who returns his gaze, but continues in flight across the path of the adult. The two figures are in communication, but leave each other quite free. The 'experienced' illustration depicts a different relationship which is more permanent but more oppressive. The piper carries the child on his head, and because he must use his hands to lend support, has abandoned his pipe. There is no communication between the two, even though they are 'tied' to each other, and situated as they are they cannot even see each other. The child, who floated without assistance, now has wings, but as he is supported by the piper and held by him, the wings are of no use to him – he is an encumbrance to the piper and the piper has deprived him of his freedom. The picture might be seen as an illustration for the first two lines of *Eternity*:

> He who bends himself a joy
> Does the winged life destroy.

The experienced piper has wanted the child instead of unselfishly appreciating him, has grasped at him, and so lost sight of the real child (who cannot act as he should), while the piper gains a burden which does not allow him to be himself. The relationship is sterile – the piper cannot pipe and the child becomes a cherub, a parody of Innocence.

In the innocent *Introduction* the piper and child can enjoy being with each other because they respect one another's independence, and each can fulfil his own being. The piper fulfils himself by making songs, first piping them, then singing them, and eventually writing them down, though in changing from the one activity to the other the same songs are uttered:

> Drop thy pipe thy happy pipe
> Sing thy songs of happy chear.
> So I sung the same again . . .

The piper moves from music to words and then to writing as though there were no distinction between these forms of expression, and, of course, they do have this in common, that they all express the same piper. The music he plays on his pipe is wordless, but is formed within his mind and expresses his sense of the harmonious, and the words he uses when singing or writing do not have their significance only because they are descriptive of a lamb, but also because they are expressive of the singer.

This is not to imply that the piper deliberately sets his harmonies to follow some musical principle, nor that he sets out, when using words, to give a deliberate account of himself. His sense of harmony underlies his tunes, his person underlies his words and, because the self-expression in his songs is unpremeditated, it is more complete than any conscious attempt at self-explanation could be. The experienced person attempts to reach a deliberate verbal understanding of himself, and in doing so substitutes an idea of himself which falsifies or obscures the movements of his spirit. The innocent singer, even in talking about himself, allows his spirit to slip into the words unintentionally so that we may apprehend what he is.

Perhaps it is a characteristic of much great poetry that, in addition to the meanings that the poet puts deliberately into his verses, the words are expressive, also, of meanings too complex to be consciously intended, because the fullness of the life of the poet is in them. In writing, the poet gives himself away, and as readers we are aware of the presence of his essential spirit in his poetry. Good poetry gives us more than a simple objective description, though we are aware of its force and truth as description. The innocence of the poet allows him to be sincere – that is, it allows him a spontaneous fullness of response to the object of his description that allows the object, too, to be fully realized. The innocence of the piper lies in his attitude to the child. He meets it, enjoys being with it and, because he has no desire to meddle with it, he sees it clearly. And at all times he fulfils himself, whether in talking to the child, in piping or in writing poems. The innocence of the poet (and the piper is presented as the writer of the *Songs of Innocence*) is similar. His poetry is a self-fulfilment, but it 'kisses the joy as it flies'; it allows the lively qualities of the things it presents us with to assert themselves and it is only by not meddling, by not distorting his experience, that the poet can be fully himself.

All of us, except the very young perhaps, place great importance on the rational interpretation and direction of the events of our world. We like to feel that we are in clear and conscious control of ourselves and of our decisions, and we labour hard to put all our knowledge in an orderly and comprehensible scheme. Blake realized the value of this attempt, but realized, also, that in order to gain rational control we are obliged to leave some things out of account so that we might give a better account of others – obliged to stereotype our world and to pretend to an omniscience we do not have. We live, to some degree, 'in disguise' because we adopt set attitudes and responses, and our world lies hidden from us because we see there only what habit and convenience prepare us to find. The *Songs of Experience* display the mind working in this limited way. At its best, however, the rational mind opens up new vistas of experience. The songs are intellectual poems and, though in the innocent *Introduction* Blake celebrates a spontaneous and 'inspired' art, his doing so is a feat of controlled thought. Despite the control, the thought is imaginative because it is indicative of Blake's originality, insight, and understanding – is indicative of his ability to let things be themselves. There is the same free relationship between himself and the subject of his verses as exists between the piper and the child.

By contrast, the relationship depicted in the *Introduction* to the *Songs of Experience* and its companion poem, *Earth's Answer*, is a frustrated one. The bard attempts to speak to Earth, but though his message is an inspired one she cannot respond because her habitual mode of thought makes her misinterpret what he says, so that she hears what she expects him to say, and not what he delivers. The bard is inspired as a prophet, not in the unpremeditated manner of the piper and, like most prophets, he goes unheeded and virtually unheard. He speaks to a fallen Earth and so speaks, not of a lamb, but of God and of regeneration, and he speaks in the manner of the seer, with weighty things to utter.

Introduction

Hear the voice of the Bard!
Who Present, Past, & Future sees
Whose ears have heard,
The Holy Word,
That walk'd among the ancient trees.

Calling the lapsed Soul,
And weeping in the evening dew:
That might controll.
The starry pole:
And fallen fallen light renew!

O Earth O Earth return!
Arise from out the dewy grass;
Night is worn.
And the morn
Rises from the slumberous mass.

Turn away no more:
Why wilt thou turn away

The starry floor
The watry shore
Is giv'n thee till the break of day.

EARTH'S *Answer*

Earth rais'd up her head,
From the darkness dread & drear.
Her light fled.
Stony dread!
And her locks cover'd with grey despair.

Prison'd on watry shore
Starry Jealousy does keep my den
Cold and hoar
Weeping o'er
I hear the father of the ancient men

Selfish father of men
Cruel jealous selfish fear
Can delight
Chain'd in night
The virgins of youth and morning bear

Does spring hide its joy
When buds and blossoms grow?
Does the sower?
Sow by night?
Or the plowman in darkness plow?

Break this heavy chain.
That does freeze my bones around
Selfish! vain.
Eternal bane!
That free Love with bondage bound.

Like the Piper, the Bard is a poet, but his poetry is prophetic, and brings a message. His 'inspiration' comes from the Divinity, he speaks with authority in the first line of the poem and, like

God, he beholds 'Present, Past & Future'. Like God, he calls to the 'lapsed Soul', and pleads with a fallen Earth to return to the way of light. He speaks on behalf of a loving God – the 'Holy Word' and the 'true light', who, according to St John, 'was made flesh and dwelt among us'; the Son who is described in *Paradise Lost* as the 'mild Judge and Intercessor' walking in the Garden in the evening of the day of the Fall. The Bard takes Milton one stage further, and describes the Word as 'weeping in the evening dew', perhaps having Christ's agony in the garden in mind, as well as the judgement of Adam and Eve.

Before the Fall, God was known to Earth, he walked among the 'ancient trees' of Eden and was the intimate of Adam and Eve until they became 'lapsed Souls'. After the Fall, however, Earth does not respond to the love of the Word or know him for what he is. In speaking of the Word, St John says that 'In him was life; and the life was the light of men' (1.4), but goes on to say 'And the light shineth in darkness; and the darkness comprehended it not' (1. 5), also 'He was in the world, and the world was made by him, and the world knew him not' (1. 10). God in not present to Earth as he is to the Bard, in the shape of one who calls and weeps. Instead he is an unseen, remote patriarch – a moody tyrant who has chained her, just as the fallen angels were 'cast down to hell, and delivered into chains of darkness, to be reserved unto judgment' (II Peter 2. 4). Her God also weeps, but not in loving kindness or regret. The tears of the Holy Word are associated with the 'evening dew', with a refreshing and rejuvenating power, while the 'Father of the ancient men' is described as 'weeping o'er' in frustration and self-pity. The Bard has attempted to tell Earth of God's mercy and grace, but she is aware only of the jealous and capricious figure, so often found in the Old Testament, whose love is possessive and who punishes his children when they are disobedient. The Bard and Earth conceive God differently and so are hopelessly at cross purposes, and when he speaks of God's grief at the Fall, and his mercy in judgement which allows of regeneration, she remembers only the strict version of Genesis in which God curses the ground for the sake of Adam's sin.

God may be known to man only as man is capable of receiving him, and so most religions, including Christianity, present more than one possible vision of the Divinity. One view, the view most often given in the *Songs of Experience*, is that of a Jehovah-like figure, a Nobodaddy who controls the universe from a vast distance according to laws which, like the movements of the stars, are fixed and only partly comprehensible. To man, his ways seem tyrannical and unpredictable and, though he is the Father, he is a stern and forbidding one. His children are ignorant, he regards their ways as evil, and they need the threat of punishment constantly held over them if they are to be controlled at all. The *Songs of Innocence* present a very different view of God. He is within the world, caring for it as described in *On Anothers Sorrow*:

> He doth give his joy to all.
> He becomes an infant small
> He becomes a man of woe
> He doth feel the sorrow too.

The speakers in the *Songs of Innocence* do not look upon our earthly state as sinful – how can it be, when God himself has assumed our condition; has become like us to share in our humanity? The innocent conceive God as a lamb or as a child because, being without a sense of guilt, they are also without fear of punishment. It is as well, perhaps, that those whose motives are less pure may choose to keep themselves in order by means of the knowledge of a God who will exact retribution for their sins.

In the *Introduction* and *Earth's Answer* Blake presents contrary ideas of God, making use of an imagery that is, in part, sexual. The illustration to the *Introduction* shows Earth as a naked woman lying with her back turned, and the Bard pleads with her:

> Turn away no more:
> Why wilt thou turn away
> The starry floor
> The watry shore
> Is giv'n thee till the break of day.

She is turned from the Bard himself, hiding her beauty from him, turned from the Holy Word, for whom the Bard speaks, and turned from what has been 'giv'n' her: the 'starry floor' and 'watry shore'. As depicted, she is beautiful, and reclines on a flowing cloth (the 'watry shore') supported on a cloud set among stars (the 'starry floor'). This 'starry floor' or 'watry shore' is the created universe, the 'firmament in the midst of the waters' of Genesis 1. 6, and her attitude towards it is one of disgust and rejection. But Earth is, herself, part of the firmament, and so this attitude is one of self-disgust, and the Bard pleads with her to recognize her own beauty, and to see that her existence is a blessing. She might awaken to the refreshment of 'dewy' morning, to the magnificence of 'The starry floor/The watry shore', and to the knowledge that these things are a gift. The 'break of day' which the Bard urges her to accept is not the start of a new life elsewhere. He has already announced the rise of morn, though Earth is not aware that it has come and rejects his statement or misunderstands it. 'Break of day' for Earth is a renewal that can only come when she changes her attitude – turns towards the light unashamed of her beauty, which is also the grace and beauty of the creation, and, in so turning, receives the admiration which is offered her. The new day is a dawning of Earth's beauty when the light comes, a dawning on earth, not away from it. But she does not respond to the plea of the Bard.

The last two stanzas of the *Introduction* are expressed in the manner of a lover, and Earth rejects the proffered love with disgust. She does not respond in the rôle the Bard hopes for: as a fulfilled and joyous woman, risen refreshed and vigorous from her own 'dewy grass', but as an old, worn, and disillusioned wife might do in accusing a husband to whom she is bound in a servile and joyless union. Love should be free, but hers has been 'with bondage bound'. The children of mother Earth are begotten furtively at night, conceived in sin and begotten in pain. She is the descendant of Eve, to whom God said: 'I will greatly multiply thy sorrow and thy conception; in sorrow thou shalt bring forth children; and thy desire shall be to thy husband, and he shall rule over thee.' Natural processes, especially the sexual process, have become ugly and shameful, not to be gone through in the light of day, but secretly, as if the sower were to 'sow by night' or the plowman were to plow 'in darkness'. Earth brings forth her children, but fathered as they are by a God anguished by a sense of the unclean, they cannot be 'virgins of youth and morning' – they never know innocence or joy, but instead are burdened with a sense of sin and shame from birth. To God, Earth attributes the qualities of a patriarch of the drearier and stricter varieties of Christianity. He is 'Starry Jealously', but the stars have lost their beauty. They do not decorate the firmament, but, in their fixed courses, are signs of the law. He broods possessively over his wife, whom he cannot leave alone but cannot delight, because his love has become a form of self-gratification. Small wonder that he is racked with a sense of guilt. His wife must submit to his embraces at night and to his preoccupation with sinfulness at all times. She is 'chained' to his lusts and revulsions, and his moral sickness has robbed her of joy in life. There is no real intercourse in such a marriage, yet neither partner is free of the other, and their life is a freezing winter of despair. To people who cannot be intimate with one another and cannot leave one another alone, God can only come (as he comes to Earth) in the shape of a remote but interfering tyrant.

God can come differently to the Bard, and the manner in which he comes is indicative of the sympathetic nature of the speaker. In the first stanza of the poem the prophet-poet speaks in a rather official tone, giving a command and announcing himself in the first line, and then going on to state his credentials. His vision is God-like, and his message is divine, for if it does not come directly from God, it is spoken by one who has heard God's voice, and so can speak with God's authority. This official voice is not maintained, however, and although the call to Earth is delivered as from God in the last two stanzas, there is a personal urgency in the appeal that comes from the Bard himself. God is Earth's lover, but so is the Bard, and the strength of his desire is felt in the reiterated cry:

> Turn away no more:
> Why wilt thou turn away . . .

51

It is difficult, in the latter half of the poem, to separate God's appeal from the Bard's, for the messenger delivers the message from his own heart. It is even more difficult to be certain, in the second stanza, who it is that calls the 'lapsed Soul' and weeps 'in the evening dew'. It might be the Word, but it might be the Bard, and Blake's punctuation does not help us to decide clearly. As the stanza proceeds, it becomes even more involved, and we are less sure of who might 'controll / The starry pole' or renew 'fallen fallen light'. It might be the Word, it might be the Bard, and it might be the Soul in its proper condition. The stanza may suggest that, if he cared to use it, the Holy Word has the power to guide the course of events on Earth just as he has established the movements of the stars, for 'All things were made by him; and without him was not anything made that was made' (John 1. 3). He could prevent the Fall and he could, at will, raise up those who have fallen, though such control would deprive his creatures of their freedom of choice. This view of God's powers would suit *Earth's Answer* but does not fit well into the *Introduction*, where the Holy Word, if he is to 'controll', does so through love and through eliciting a response, not through force or the imposition of his will. Control here does not imply dominance, but the mutual participation of beings who are free to work together and have regard for one another. The ambiguities in the stanza are designed to emphasize this meaning of the word 'control'. God may work through the Bard only because the Bard consents and gives his own strength to the appeal, speaking God's word by speaking as himself, not as one who makes pronouncements on behalf of a mysterious supernatural being. The call to the 'lapsed Soul' comes from the Word and it comes also from the Bard, though not because they are identical but because of the attraction that is between them and the purpose which unites them in their attraction to the Earth. God and Bard control one another in their relationship, though there is no question of dominance, only of increasing the vitality, each one of the other, unlike the control complained of in *Earth's Answer* where God who dominates, no less than Earth, who is dominated, is enslaved in an isolated misery. The Word, then:

might controll.
The starry pole:
And fallen fallen light renew

only with the consent and participation of the Soul. In responding to God, the Soul might transform itself, but God, too, needs transformation if he is to be more than a 'Starry Jealousy'. If man falls into selfishness and confusion then God, as he is known, falls with him, and can be renewed only by the understanding of the Soul. The Fall is spoken of with infinite regret by the Bard, and the repetition of 'fallen' emphasizes the continuing nature of the separation and decline, the lack of control which neither party can regain alone. In their separation the Word and the Soul are impotent. Because they may become properly themselves only in mutual understanding and sympathy, Blake does not specify who might 'controll / The starry pole'. In isolation Word and Soul have no purpose, but together they give significance to the universe.

The Bard might 'controll' too, if he could elicit a response, for he does not speak as a mere mouthpiece for an absolute being beyond time and space. Instead he calls to Earth on his own behalf, as a lover would, asking her to come to a knowledge of her beauty through a realization of his desire. The Earth cannot understand that by speaking in this manner he speaks in the rôle of God, by showing the divine impulses to pity and love. The idea would be blasphemous to her because she can only think of the Divine in a superstitious way as a supernatural, mysterious potentate to whom she must be either servile, or show opposition. She cannot understand, and so her speech is separated from that of the Bard in a second poem. They communicate by means of apparently related monologues, though on different subjects really; and there can be no real concurrence, as exists between Word and Bard, whose words are blended by Blake in one poem to indicate a better relationship.

Blake makes use, in the two poems we have been studying, as he does in many of the songs, of overtones of sexual imagery in order to make his purpose clear. In sexual love we declare our

53

innocence or lack of it very plainly, depending on how selfless we can be. Sympathy, admiration of another, spontaneous self-forgetfulness are the proper characteristics of love of all kinds, as they are the characteristics of all innocent relationships, and these qualities are shown in the Bard's song. He acts in such close harmony with the Word that he speaks selflessly, making the desire of God his own desire, though this is a fulfilment of his person, not a sacrifice of individuality. Blake indicates this poetically by allowing the Bard's voice first to blend with God's voice and then to take over God's speaking voice entirely. The Bard (and so the Word) speaks to Earth with the urgency of a lover, though she misunderstands the nature of the love that is offered, assuming that it is of the experienced kind: a mutual compact for self-gratification, which ends in disgust and recrimination. The fall undergone by Earth, her lapse into Exerience, is an event that has affected every aspect of her thought, including the sexual and the religious aspects, and Blake brings these two fields together in order to elucidate the nature of the decline in each, and in order to show the collapse of the whole person. One of the *Songs of Experience*, *A Little Girl Lost* deals directly with the moment of the fall from Innocence to Experience, and in that song too, religious and sexual aspects are associated, though the poem deals primarily with the sexual.

A Little GIRL Lost

Children of the future Age.
Reading this indignant page ;
Know that in a former time.
Love! sweet Love! was thought a crime.

In the Age of Gold,   5
Free from winters cold:
Youth and maiden bright
To the holy light.
Naked in the sunny beams delight.

Once a youthful pair   10
Fill'd with softest care:

Met in garden bright.
Where the holy light.
Had just remov'd the curtains of the night.

There in rising day.   15
On the grass they play:
Parents were afar:
Strangers came not near:
And the maiden soon forgot her fear.

Tired with kisses sweet   20
They agree to meet.
When the silent sleep
Waves o'er heavens deep:
And the weary tired wanderers weep.

To her father white   25
Came the maiden bright:
But his loving look.
Like the holy book.
All her tender limbs with terror shook.

Ona! pale and weak!   30
To thy father speak:
O the trembling fear!
O the dismal care!
That shakes the blossoms of my hoary hair

In most of the songs Blake simply presents us with a statement
made by an imaginary speaker, and leaves the reader to pass
judgement on what is said. His two nurses, for instance, speak in
their own voices, and we are invited to compare their statements
in order to decide what sort of person makes each one. In *A
Little Girl Lost*, however, the poet has taken the rôle of narrator.
He describes a series of events in the body of the poem, and re-
ports the words of the father in the last stanza, all without comment, but he does allow himself to speak in the introductory stanza.
The poem tells us about Ona's fall from Innocence, which takes
place, not on the occasion of her sexual encounter with the youth,

but as the result of her father's 'loving look'. He is a 'child' of the present age, and in the present age, so we are reminded in the introductory stanza, 'Love! sweet Love' is 'thought a crime'. Ona, too, is a child of the present age, and like Earth in *Earth's Answer*, cannot avoid being infected by the sense of guilt associated with sexual matters. Blake addresses the 'Children of the future Age' who will have accepted the invitation of the Bard, and will have ceased to 'turn away' in disgust. They will share Blake's indignation, presumably, when they read the sad tale of Ona, which is the story of all 'children' of the present, although their indignation will be mixed with a sense of disbelief that such a state of affairs could exist, or so the stanza implies. For a 'child' of the present age it is difficult to believe that 'Children of the future Age' will live in a permanent state of innocence, and they are, of course, hypothetical beings, introduced by Blake in order to emphasize the absurdity of the position in the present. No child who continued in unspoiled innocence could share Blake's indignation, or have the least idea of what he was talking about – and an age of unspoiled innocence does not seem imminent, or even possible for mankind. If Blake is writing history for a 'future Age' he writes it in the certain knowledge that its children will share the inevitable conditions of human existence and that they, too, will undergo the fall. In the body of the poem he writes history for children of the present time, and tells the story of Adam and Eve, modifying it so that it is the history of every man and woman. The story is timeless, and in order to indicate its timelessness Blake slips from one tense to another as he writes. The first stanza in the body of the poem is about a past event, set in an 'Age of Gold', but is written in the present tense to indicate that Eden is enacted in every person's experience. We are meant to think of the Garden planted by the Lord God where 'they were both naked, the man and his wife, and were not ashamed', and the 'light' is the 'holy' light of the new creation. But the myth is a universal one, and so Blake refers to the time, also, as the classical 'Age of Gold' when 'men of their own accord, without threat of punishment, without laws, maintained good faith and did what was right' (Ovid, *Metamorphoses* I). We are in the apparently endless spring of the early world and view the apparently permanent innocence of young life.

In the second stanza Blake slips into the past tense in order to emphasize the fact that, by the end of the poem, Ona has lost her innocence, though the loss is not due to her physical experience. Her fall is brought about by a single 'looking look' directed at her by her father. Blake is not chronicling a past event, however. Ona is not, like Eve, a single person, but is representative of all men and women, and the fall is not a single event in our lives, but may be undergone in any situation. The possibility always exists, in any of our relationships, that we may enjoy the experience in self-forgetful appreciation, though as we leave our infancy and early childhood further behind, the more likely we become to distort our experiences in an attempt to bend them to our ideas of what they should be. The fall takes place throughout our lives in the succession of our failures, and to indicate the continuing nature of the process Blake addresses the future and writes in past and present tenses. In the third stanza he changes from the present to the past after the second line, the fourth stanza is written in the present tense, and the fifth reverts to the past. Blake's poem, ostensibly written as history, is an account of man at any time and applies to each one of us at any moment of our lives.

Milton's Adam and Eve, like the 'youthful pair' of this poem, are innocent before they fall, and they are not ignorant. They know what it is to work in the garden, and they know each other sexually, but after they lapse their work becomes a labour, and their innocent knowledge of each other becomes tinged with feelings of guilt and shame. Their activities do not change, but their attitude towards those activities makes them into something different. Ona, too, is not ignorant, but her knowledge is altered when she meets her father. He divines that something has taken place, and his look of distrust and fear infects her knowledge even before he speaks, so that she too shakes with terror and goes pale. The father's look is 'like the holy book' because it is fraught with the awful prohibitions and repressions imposed on himself by fallen man to control his distorted impulses. 'Thou shalt not' is written as plainly on the face of the father as it is written in Exodus. There is no need for him to explain Ona's 'sin', though no doubt he will attempt to do so – she feels her guilt, and is no longer the same person who promised to meet her lover:

> When the silent sleep
> Waves o'er heavens deep:
> And the weary tired wanderers weep.

She might meet him, but for neither of them will the meeting be what they had anticipated, as her new wisdom will infect him too. By the lines just quoted, Blake means, perhaps, that the lovers knew that life was not all uncomplicated joy in a deserted garden – they knew that there is frustration, wandering and weeping, but had supposed that there would always be consolation in their meetings. They did not know that even this consolation could become a thing of sorrow and confusion.

Blake indicates the universality of the situation he describes by slipping unobtrusively from one tense to another. His indication of the insidious nature of the change that takes place with the fall is indicated in an equally subtle manner. Words that are used in the first part of the poem are repeated towards the end, the repetition is given prominence by the placing of these words at the end of lines in a rhyming position, and the rhyme scheme, with its frequent echoes, also throws the words into prominence. Thus 'care' at the end of line 11 occurs again at the end of the second last line, though a very different sort of 'care' is implied in the new context. The 'softest care' of the youthful couple with its implication of tenderness and mutual regard becomes the 'dismal care' of the father, with its attendant fear and distrust. The young people are 'Fill'd' with their care. It flows spontaneously over, while the father's care is 'dismal' because it is a nagging anxiety elaborated in his own mind and forced on his daughter. His 'fear' in the previous line (line 32) is of the same sort. It is 'trembling' – an anticipation of evil that is unhealthy, selfish, even greedy for the worst in a perverted way. He induces a fear in Ona that is quite different to the 'fear' she feels earlier in the poem: 'And the maiden soon forgot her fear' (line 19). That was a healthy fear in response to a strange circumstance and could be dispelled, but the fear instilled by her father is a vague moral fear that will continue to influence her always. The word 'holy' is also repeated, occurring first in lines 8 and 13 in association with 'light', and again in line 28 with 'book'. The 'light' is holy because it is divine – the first creation of God which 'remov'd the curtains of the night'. Light is a gift, and unfallen man worships God as the giver, and as one who 'cares' for us (in the innocent sense of the word). Fallen man pays homage to God as the law giver, the prohibitor and the punisher, and the 'holy book' is the Old Testament record of the visitations of the terrifying being who 'cares' for us (in the experienced sense of the word). The book is 'holy' because it is mysteriously disclosed, is to be held in awe, and contains the authority of a being greater than ourselves.

In the first three stanzas there are numerous references to light. The 'Age of Gold' is a time of spring, of early morning and of 'sunny beams'. The light is 'holy', for God has seen that it is good, the maiden is 'bright', and the day rises as the young persons mature. By contrast, there is whiteness at the end of the poem, but it is without warmth, being associated with fear and restriction. Ona's father is 'white', and she becomes 'pale'. In the last line we are outside the 'garden bright', being left with the shaking of the 'blossoms' of the father's 'hoary hair'. These flowers are frosty and sterile, and they cannot wither as the 'garden' has done. The delicate equilibrium of Innocence has been disturbed, and the fall is now complete.

Blake is sometimes regarded as an advocate of unrestrained sexual love as a way to fuller living; so it is, perhaps, necessary to point out that though *A Little Girl Lost* asks us to think about our state, and helps us to define one of the conditions of human life, it offers no remedy for the state of Experience. That state must be encountered with the resources of Experience, imperfect though they are. 'Free love' is possible, perhaps, in a state of Innocence, but for experienced man to suppose that he can return voluntarily to that state is to assume what is not possible. What may be spontaneously done by the innocent cannot be deliberately copied in Experience, and the very act of longing for the freedoms possible to Innocence is indicative of the fallen mind. Innocence gives praise for the conditions of its existence by accepting them, like the Piper and like the Bard. Guilt and frustration, like that of Earth or of Ona's father, belong to Experience, and may be associated with the setting up of a formula for self-improvement, but such formulae are certain to fail if they advocate an imitation of Innocence.

4

SYMPATHY IN INNOCENCE
AND IN EXPERIENCE

Innocence is wholly engrossed in its activities, is self-forgetful, though self-fulfilled, and its sympathies are whole-hearted. The sympathies of Experience, on the other hand, are self-centred, deliberate and involve the feelings in a limited way. Experienced man, looking into his own mind, concludes quite rightly that sympathy arises from fear or selfishness. We feel for the sufferer, he says, because we recognize his pain as one that might be visited also on us, and we like to give pleasure to others because we like the feeling of being magnanimous or because we hope for a return of pleasure. The sympathy of lovers is a means of obtaining mutual gratification, and there is some personal gratification in relieving the distresses we encounter. Despite the apparent meaning of the word – to suffer with – our 'sympathetic' feelings do not correspond with those that exist in the breast of the person we feel for, though, as his feelings are the cue for our own, we like to think that they are the same. This correspondence, says Experience, is impossible, feelings cannot be transferred in that way, our emotions are entirely self-possessed, and our pains and pleasures cannot be known by another. This account of sympathy is true, no doubt, for most of us in most of the encounters of our lives, but there are moments, more frequent in persons we designate 'innocent', when we are clenched less rigidly in the grasp of our self-regard and will, when our hearts are more vulnerable, and we sympathize in a better sense of the word. Such moments are difficult to describe. Innocence does not attempt to analyse itself and, when recollected, the moment is examined by a mind no longer acting spontaneously. We may be aware that the moment was a gracious one but, in describing it, be obliged to apply the mechanical terms of Experience. Innocence tends to defy rational analysis – its doings are distorted by explanation – and a poetic statement of its qualities is much more full and flexible, as we have seen in the case of the songs of the innocent nurse and chimney sweeper, in *Infant Joy* and the innocent *Holy Thursday*. The *Songs of Innocence* all imply that a better type of sympathy is possible than that asserted in the *Songs of Experience*, though both descriptions are true ones because the human mind is capable of both states of feeling. Blake does not, in fact, use the word 'sympathy', for the same reason that he very seldom uses the word 'love'. Both terms have become too closely associated with the emotions known to Experience; they are one-sided, and Blake prefers to use such words as 'care', which retain their flexibility, giving various meanings in various contexts. Blake's most successful poetic depiction of innocent sympathy is achieved in *A Cradle Song*, one of the *Songs of Innocence*, which we shall examine together with a poem which he never printed, but which is found written in his *Notebook* (sometimes called the Rossetti Manuscript). This poem bears the same title and is obviously an experienced counterpart of the printed poem.

A CRADLE SONG

Sweet dreams form a shade.
O'er my lovely infants head.
Sweet dreams of pleasant streams.
By happy silent moony beams

Sweet sleep with soft down.   5
Weave thy brows an infant crown.
Sweet sleep Angel mild,
Hover o'er my happy child.

Sweet smiles in the night.
Hover over my delight.   10
Sweet smiles Mothers smiles
All the livelong night beguiles.

Sweet moans. dovelike sighs,
Chase not slumber from thy eyes.
Sweet moans. sweeter smiles.   15
All the dovelike moans beguiles.

Sleep sleep happy child.
All creation slept and smil'd.
Sleep sleep. happy sleep.
While o'er thee thy mother weep   20

Sweet babe in thy face.
Holy image I can trace.
Sweet babe once like thee.
Thy maker lay and wept for me

Wept for me for thee for all.   25
When he was an infant small.
Thou his image ever see.
Heavenly face that smiles on thee.

Smiles on thee on me on all.
Who became an infant small.   30
Infant smiles are his own smiles.
Heaven & earth to peace beguiles.

A CRADLE SONG

Sleep, Sleep, beauty bright
Dreaming o'er the joys of night
Sleep, Sleep: in thy sleep
Little sorrows sit & weep.

Sweet Babe, in thy face   5
Soft desires I can trace
Secret joys & secret smiles
Little pretty infant wiles

As thy softest limbs I feel
Smiles as of the morning steal   10
O'er thy cheek & o'er thy breast
Where thy little heart does rest.

O, the cunning wiles that creep
In thy little heart asleep.
When thy little heart does wake,   15
Then the dreadful lightnings break.

From thy cheek & from thy eye
O'er the youthful harvests nigh
Infant wiles & infant smiles
Heaven & Earth of peace beguiles.   20

Both poems depict a mother watching over her sleeping infant. The mothers use a similar vocabulary, and such words as 'sweet', 'weep', 'soft', 'peace', and 'beguiles' are found in each song, although Blake, in his usual manner, expects us to see the contrasts made by these words in their different settings. The last lines of the two songs, for instance, duplicate each other except for a single preposition, and Blake has made the least possible alteration to achieve a large difference in meaning. The innocent infant beguiles 'to peace' – he wins heaven and earth by soothing them; while the experienced song describes heaven and earth being fraudulently deprived of their peace – they are beguiled 'of peace'. Both mothers admire their babies, but in very different ways. The first speaks of her 'lovely infant' (line 2), in terms which emphasize the personal and subjective nature of her admiration, while the second addresses the child as 'beauty bright', making a more assertive statement attributing an impersonal and absolute value to the looks of the baby.

The innocent mother is much more tentative in all her statements than her more dogmatic sister. The latter comes close to commanding her baby to sleep:

Sleep, Sleep, beauty bright
Dreaming o'er the joys of night . . .

Sleep is seen as an activity voluntarily undertaken, and she speaks to the child as though he were an adult, not unlike herself. She knows what goes on in his mind – he dreams, and in those dreams experiences 'joys' and 'sorrows'. She can trace the 'soft desires' read on the baby's face and sees that he is gratified by her caresses. She knows, also, that he encourages the caresses and other joys by means of 'wiles' – ways calculated to charm the response he wants. The mother is like the speaker in *Infant Sorrow* (pp. 1–4) who can give a full account of the inward processes of the infant because he sees mirrored there an exact replica of his own mind. As the mother projects her own feelings and motives into the infant she can hardly fail to 'sympathize' with what she has put there.

On a superficial view, it might appear that the innocent mother is more distant from her child. She refuses to assert anything about his inward processes, and sees sleep, not as a state of his being, but as a 'crown' on the brows of the child or as an 'Angel' hovering over him. He is not said to dream, but the dreams are a 'shade' over his head, and he does not smile, but the smiles 'hover over' him like the 'Angel' of sleep. She does not penetrate further than these outward manifestations, and they do not appear to emanate from the child, but rather to descend upon him. She cannot read his soul, and so when she talks of his dreams she calls them from elsewhere as a benediction on her baby and cannot state that he experiences them. Her heart yearns to the child, she desires all good for him, but he is an utter stranger to her and she knows nothing about him beyond his appearance. She does not find categories of 'joy' and 'sorrow' for the emotions of the infant because it does not occur to her to wonder about what lies beneath the manifestations she observes. She is content with what is given to her eye and ear, and when she describes the baby as 'happy child' (lines 8 and 17) the words refer to her own feelings of good fortune and contentment and do not attempt to describe the baby's emotions. The child is 'happy' because he is blessed, and so his sleep is also called 'happy' in line 19.

There is an unpleasantly voluptuous element in the experienced mother's satisfaction in her infant's body, also in her vicarious relish of his supposed enjoyments and anticipations of pleasure. She gratifies herself, and by doing so gratifies the child who encourages the sensual delights he has gained:

> As thy softest limbs I feel
> Smiles as of the morning steal
> O'er thy cheek & o'er thy breast
> Where thy little heart does rest.

Her fondling of the limbs of the baby comes very close to being a sexual indulgence, especially as the child's reception and encouragement of the caresses is seen as a preparation for 'youthful harvests nigh' (line 18). At the moment the child responds with smiles which ensure a continuation of the caresses, though the smiles are less innocent than they appear to be – they are '*as* of the morning', and they 'steal' from the baby, being furtive and slightly indecent. They are an outcome of the 'cunning wiles that creep / In thy little heart asleep' (lines 13 and 14), for in his primitive way the child calculates how to get what he wants, though he keeps his intentions well hidden. He provides enjoyments for his mother and flatters her with 'smiles', though his real purpose in doing so is to receive enjoyments for himself. At the moment the 'little heart' of the baby is at 'rest'. He is a fairly passive recipient of his pleasures, only smiling to encourage them, though when he wakes he will take delights more actively, and most actively when he leaves infancy behind and becomes more capable of reaping his 'youthful harvests'. Then the 'dreadful lightnings break' (line 20). Pleasures may be taken more ruthlessly, the will of the individual be asserted with greater mastery, and energy and desire consummated in a violent outburst that expends them. At the moment, however, these outbursts are anticipated (not necessarily consciously), or are being prepared for, and what the mother projects on to the face of her baby are 'soft desires' (line 6) and 'Secret joys and secret smiles', though these are no mystery to her. In all the descriptions of the child as seen by the experienced mother there is an implicit theory of the cunning, selfishness and greed of our motives, though we ensure the most gratification to ourselves if we behave in a way that gratifies other persons. Even in the baby, most helpless and unformed of human beings, the mother sees a rudimentary capacity for calculation and determination associated with appetites not very different from her own, and with methods of achievement familiar to Experience.

If the innocent mother can be said to feel sympathy with her child it is not because she puts in his place a replica of herself, to which response is inevitable. She does not suppose that she can fathom her baby, and this enables her to establish a much closer

feeling for him than we have seen in the experienced poem.
Stanzas 3 and 4 indicate this very clearly:

> Sweet smiles in the night.　　　　　9
> Hover over my delight.
> Sweet smiles Mothers smiles
> All the livelong night beguiles.　　　12
>
> Sweet moans. dovelike sighs,
> Chase not slumber from thy eyes.
> Sweet moans. sweeter smiles.
> All the dovelike moans beguiles.　　　16

The lines are in the form of a benediction, and a hope that the
infant may sleep undisturbed, despite the 'moans' and 'sighs'
(line 13) which he utters, and which indicate unrest. Even the
moans of the child are sweet to her, but the child's smiles are
'sweeter' because they beguile away the 'dovelike moans' (line
16). In the first of the two stanzas she summons 'smiles' to hover
over the face of the child and adds the protection of her own smiles,
beguiling peace upon him. This is one way of reading the lines,
but they are highly ambiguous. The smiles that hover over the
child (line 10) may be those that are seen on his face, but may also
be those on the face of the mother as she hovers over his cradle.
Lines 11 and 12 may describe the infant beguiled to rest by his
own smiles and his mother's, but it may be his mother who is
beguiled as she watches. In lines 13 and 14 the mother may hope
that the baby will not be awakened by his moans and smiles or
she may hope that her own moans and smiles will not disturb
him. It is impossible to say, when reading lines 15 and 16, who
beguiles whom: the mother's utterances, if they are hers, may
beguile the child or beguile herself, or the utterances may be those
of the child who beguiles himself or beguiles his mother. These
ambiguities are deliberately placed in the poem by Blake, and we
are meant to accept all the possibilities, not because the speaker is
showing a conscious verbal dexterity, but because she is so engrossed in the child that she has ceased to make the differentiations

we make when more self-collected. She attends so closely to the manifestations on the child's face, and her own expressions follow so responsively and spontaneously what she sees there, that it is clear that she is lost in her companionship with him. She is hardly aware of her baby's motions as belonging beyond herself, they move so directly into her own soul – though, as we have seen, she does not presume to understand more of the child than this bond of responsiveness establishes in her. Indeed she is not conscious of 'responding' at all. The 'smiles' and 'moans' hover between mother and child (just as 'sleep' and 'dreams' hover over him), and she is hardly aware of who is responsible for these manifestations, being as innocent of thoughts of her own personality as she is of thoughts about the personality of the child.

By means of the ambiguities in the two stanzas we have just examined, Blake poetically depicts a state of selfless absorption that defies easy statement in prose, and in the rest of the poem he goes on to extend these ambiguities into a wider sphere so as to show that the sympathy or love shown by this mother may include 'Heaven & earth', beguiling them 'to peace'. She compares her baby to the infant Christ:

> Sweet babe in thy face.   21
> Holy image I can trace.
> Sweet babe once like thee.
> Thy maker lay and wept for me . . .

God made man in his image, and so men resemble him. The innocent child is holy for that reason, but the mother is reminded, also, that God became man, and lay like her child, in pity for our fallen condition, and his tears were shed for all human kind. The mother sees the image of God in her infant, but the baby sees the divine image always:

> Thou his image ever see.   27
> Heavenly face that smiles on thee.

The child is always in the presence of his Creator, as we all are, for

God 'Smiles on thee on me on all' (line 29), but if the mother can trace God's image in the face of the infant, he, in his turn, sees God's image in her face as it bends over his cradle. The 'Heavenly face that smiles' on the baby is also the loving countenance of the speaker. Christ wept and smiled as a baby, and he wept and smiled as a man, displaying the fulness of human emotions. The mother, too, weeps and smiles over her baby, displaying emotions that are both human and divine.

The mother sees the image of God in her child, the child views it in his mother, God smilingly sees his image in both mother and child; and as we read the poem these alternatives are presented simultaneously in such lines as 'Thou his image ever see' (line 27). There is a further degree of complexity. As the child views his mother he sees also his earthly father at the time of procreation:

> Sweet babe once like thee.   23
> Thy maker lay and wept for me
>
> Wept for me for thee for all.
> When he was an infant small.

The baby has another maker who showed love at the time of his creative act and, as Blake brings to the poem the love of the mother, of God, of creation, and of salvation, he brings in, also, the love of the sexes. The weeping in these lines is a weeping in fulness of emotion, and Blake describes the sexual act after its culmination when the father has become an 'infant small', beguiled to peace at a time when 'all creation slept and smiled' (line 18). That moment came when the created world saw the sleep of the infant Christ, it comes to the mother in her present contentment as she views her baby, and it came to the earthly father and mother after their act of creation, for all these moments are times of sympathy and of selfless satisfaction. In the countenance of the baby, the mother sees, also, the image of his father, and in looking at his mother the child sees, in her delighted countenance, an image of his father at the time when love had made it a 'Heavenly face' (line 28) that smiled on her. The peace that she experienced on that occasion is the peace that she feels now, so that:

Infant smiles are his own smiles.   31
Heaven & earth to peace beguiles.

Both the experienced and innocent *Cradle Songs* have a sexual dimension, but from the experienced song it may be inferred that sexual encounters, like all encounters of experienced love, are compacts of mutual gratification made between persons with similar motives. Innocent love, on the other hand, is between persons who make no assumptions about the other, knowing nothing about motives and being perfectly content with manifestations. The innocent mother makes no statement about her infants' mind. She knows enough about God in being aware of his love. And she merely expresses the peace she has enjoyed with her husband. The experienced partners are ignorant of each other really, despite their assured knowledge, for they merely read themselves into the beloved. They cannot forget themselves, and so never experience a true involvement with another being. Innocent loves are unselfish and take delight in the presence and the delights of another. Their whole attention is given to the other, and yet they do not attempt to meddle. They are self-forgetful, yet that forgetfulness is the necessary condition of self-fulfilment.

The absorbed attention of the innocent mother is conveyed in the innocent song by the ambiguities of stanzas 3 and 4, and the ambiguities are increased, without ever becoming perplexing, in the remainder of the poem, where mother, baby, father and Christ are often interchangeable. There is more than one occasion on which 'All creation slept and smil'd' (line 18), more than one 'maker' (line 24), many 'holy images', and various occasions of 'peace' for 'Heaven & earth'. The ambiguities do not indicate that the mother (or Blake) cannot differentiate or that she assumes that the child is its father and that both are Christ. There is no merging of persons, but she simply does not categorize in the way of her experienced counterpart. All the occasions she describes were times of unselfish love – the same spirit hovered between the lovers because they had given up their tight self-control. The lightning flash of will was replaced by the energy springing from intimacy. They were periods of grace, as the present occasion is, and the same gentle inspiration is seen to be working through all these times. The influence belongs to both persons, but is forced by neither, and is creative in both. The individuals have their own privacies, but in the sympathies felt the privacies have become secondary to the uniting experience, and this is common to all the relationships depicted.

The sympathy which results in the complete absorption of the faculties of the sympathizer in the manifestations of feeling of another, to the point where feelings are apparently shared, is an essential characteristic of Innocence, just as a denial of this possibility, explicitly or implicitly made, is indicative of Experience. Innocence is seldom explicit, being content, like the innocent mother, to utter itself without making abstract statements, but in *On Anothers Sorrow*, one of the few songs where an innocent declaration of faith is made, the argument turns on the assertion that sympathy is a positive and important force among men. The poem is about the nature of God, yet it is curiously rational and experimental and never ventures into the realm of the supernatural. It is, oddly enough, the experienced thinker who, for all his hard-headed realism, resorts to recondite explanations in his account of God. Innocence deals with evidence and deduction.

On Anothers Sorrow

Can I see anothers woe.
And not be in sorrow too.
Can I see anothers grief.
And not seek for kind relief.

Can I see a falling tear.   5
And not feel my sorrows share.
Can a father see his child.
Weep. nor be with sorrow fill'd.

Can a mother sit and hear.
An infant groan an infant fear –   10
No no never can it be.
Never never can it be.

And can he who smiles on all
Hear the wren with sorrows small.
Hear the small birds grief & care   15
Hear the woes that infants bear –

And not sit beside the nest
Pouring pity in their breast.
And not sit the cradle near
Weeping tear on infants tear.   20

And not sit both night & day.
Wiping all our tears away.
O! no never can it be.
Never never can it be.

He doth give his joy to all.   25
He becomes an infant small
He becomes a man of woe
He doth feel the sorrow too.

Think not. thou canst sigh a sigh.
And thy maker is not by.   30
Think not, thou canst weep a tear.
And thy maker is not near.

O! he gives to us his joy.
That our grief he may destroy
Till our grief is fled & gone   35
He doth sit by us and moan

The opening two lines of the poem, taken alone, might be a
statement of experienced sympathy, for the sorrow felt in response
to 'anothers woe' may bear no resemblance to his emotion – it
may be self-centred. As we continue with the poem, however, it
becomes clear that the speaker takes it for granted that our fellow-
feeling may create a very close bond indeed, and the 'sorrow' of
line 2 is a very similar emotion to the 'woe' of line 1. The sight of
'anothers grief' (line 3) compels the sympathizer to 'seek for kind
relief' because his own distress is bound in with that of the sufferer

so closely that, in relieving another he relieves, also, his own pain. On line 6, 'sorrows' are spoken of as shared, and the father who sees his child 'weep' (line 7) is 'fill'd' with sorrow – is completely taken over by compassion. The distress of the mother is even more urgent:

> Can a mother sit and hear.   9
> An infant groan an infant fear –

She cannot hear the cries of her baby in indifference, but the lines imply more: she cannot be objective in the matter and the cries arouse such an urgent need for response that her ears do not simply record them, as neutral sounds might be registered. They become a matter of inward urgency. God 'smiles on all', as he did in *A Cradle Song* (p. 62) and cannot simply 'hear' the sufferings of even the smallest creature. Cries of distress become a matter of inward urgency to him as he sits in distress and pity 'beside the nest' or 'near the cradle' (stanza 5), so that he weeps with the infant and waits 'Wiping all our tears away' (line 22). It is not clear whose tears he wipes away, for, in his involvement, the weeping of the child has become the cause of his own tears.

The first three stanzas discuss human sympathy, and the next three divine sympathy, but no sudden leap is made, only an orderly step, and the last three stanzas justify the transition. The Incarnation has demonstrated God's capacity for sympathy, for he too 'becomes an infant small' (line 26), and 'becomes a man of woe', to suffer all that human kind can undergo. As in other *Songs of Innocence*, the Nativity and Incarnation, events which are significant for all ages, are spoken of in the present tense. In Christ, God demonstrated quite clearly that he was not an aloof and remote power, but a being who is prepared to share our lot by becoming one of us. Christ is the type of all sympathy and he is compelled, as we are all compelled when viewing grief, to take on ourselves the pain of feeling for and responding with the sufferer. The Incarnation is seen as an incontrovertible fact, and the logic of the poem rests partly on that fact.

The poem as a whole is a structure of orderly deductions built upon clear and indisputable knowledge, so clear to the speaker that he cannot be mistaken in his conclusions. The Incarnation, which is presented as an historical fact, is part of that knowledge, observation contributes the remainder, and the whole is presented as evidence in a very systematic way. The poem falls into three sections of three stanzas each. The first two sections have the same form: a number of questions are asked, and a definite answer is found in the last two lines, nearly identical in each section:

> No no never can it be.
> Never never can it be.

The last section of the poem, especially the last two stanzas, draws conclusions from the remainder.

Although the first two sections are devoted, for the most part, to questions, the tone is not an interrogative one. They are asked because the speaker is certain of the answers. He is rehearsing the evidence to see what he can be quite sure of so that he can go about his exposition with confidence. First he examines himself, because his own heart is most easily known, and then proceeds to an examination of parental affection, which he may know by experience and observation. He then makes a decisive statement before going on to a new section, necessarily more conjectural because dealing with the divine not the human, but once again he finds he can return the same reliable answer. The certainty with which he returns it springs partly from the fact of the Incarnation, which is referred to in the succeeding stanza, and partly from the knowledge given in the first section of the poem. If men have benign impulses, then God who gave them must be possessed of them too. It is, after all, impossible to know anything of God except what he has instilled in man, and so it is in the better part of ourselves that we must look to see what he is like. The speaker knows nothing of mystery. He does not vex his mind with the hidden mechanics of the supernatural, like the speaker in *The Tyger*, and he turns his attention to that part of the universe he is competent to examine in order to resolve his questions – turns to examine his own experience, and bases his conclusions on that.

It should be noticed, however, that the speaker does not attempt to identify God and man. Like the innocent mother in *A Cradle Song* (p. 62) who makes no claim to know her infant's mind, Blake's persona allows God his privacy. He is dealt with in a separate section (though in the third section Christ is discussed as both God and man), and the speaker deals with the attributes of God he can be sure of, without suggesting that he has probed the matter further than that. In the last two stanzas God is described as giver and as a participator in our griefs. The speaker has established these divine attributes by a process of deduction based on firm knowledge and observation. It does not occur to him to go further than this careful process takes him, and he asks no further questions. Had his observations been different – had he been unable, for instance, to find the capacity for fellow feeling in the human soul – then his conclusions would have been different and God would be differently disclosed to him. Also, had his mind been more impatient – had he wished to challenge the existence of grief and pain in the order of things, or had he wished to know more about God than observation and deduction would tell him – then a more mysterious figure would have emerged, and it would have been necessary to be more dogmatic in establishing the attributes of the Divinity.

In the *Songs of Experience* God is conceived in different ways, most of them superstitious, some fearful, some hostile and some disbelieving. We will examine some of the ways later, confining ourselves, for the present, to a further study of the conception of God seen in *On Anothers Sorrow*. Innocent religious notions are modest, but firmly understood. In *On Anothers Sorrow* the Deity is not named, being accepted merely as 'he who smiles on all'. The speaker has established the attributes of God, and rests content with having done so. The same approach, the same careful dialectic, and the same caution are seen in a religious song, more abstract in its manner, called *The Divine Image*, one of the *Songs of Innocence*.

The Divine Image

To Mercy Pity Peace and Love.
All pray in their distress:

75

And to these virtues of delight
Return their thankfulness.

For Mercy Pity Peace and Love.
Is God our father dear:
And Mercy Pity Peace and Love,
Is Man his child and care.

For Mercy has a human heart
Pity. a human face:
And Love, the human form divine.
And Peace. the human dress.

Then every man of every clime.
That prays in his distress.
Prays to the human form divine
Love Mercy Pity Peace.

And all must love the human form.
In heathen, turk or jew.
Where Mercy, Love & Pity dwell.
There God is dwelling too.

The style of the poem, like that of *On Anothers Sorrow*, is expository, logical, and so moderate that the speaker is able to make firm, confident statements without being in the least dogmatic. Its reasonable manner is heightened by the way in which one stanza follows from another. Stanza 1 makes a statement for our consideration, and the next two stanzas, which begin with 'For', substantiate the statement. The last two stanzas are introduced by 'Then', because the speaker goes on to draw certain conclusions from what he has established. We may also look on the poem as an extended syllogism, followed by a corollary. If men pray to the 'virtues of delight', as the first stanza states, and if these virtues compose the 'human form divine', as we are told in the third stanza, then the conclusion drawn in stanza 4 – that men pray to the 'human form divine' – must follow. The last stanza adds further conclusions which stem from the proof just given. There is nothing conjectural about the poem: the speaker is quite sure of his premises, he extends his enquiry just as far as a strictly rational method of argument will allow, and he goes no further than that.

The purpose of the song is to disclose the nature of the divine, but it does not do so by citing supernatural or theological authority. *On Anothers Sorrow* leaned partly on a knowledge of the scriptural Christ, but there is no reference, here, to revealed fact or historical fact. There is no appeal to any orthodox tradition whatever and, instead, the speaker gives his propositions an empirical basis. Revealed knowledge, as it is normally understood, comes only once, and only to selected individuals who pass it on to their fellows and descendants. But this speaker bases his faith on what may be revealed to any man. If we are to know that God is good we cannot be secure in that knowledge by taking it on hearsay, but only by testing our own good impulses. We can know nothing of God as Creator, though we do know his creation, and the part of the creation we really know well is within ourselves. Then why should we commit the folly of pretending to wisdom we do not have, making confident statements about the realm of the super-natural, as religious thinkers are so inclined to do, when we can, with good sense and a proper humility, examine whatever is divine as it lies at hand? If we can confidently say that 'Mercy Pity Peace and Love, / Is Man', then it is not unreasonable to say the same about God, though that statement does not entitle us to make any further assumption. And if we can know no more about the Deity than that 'Mercy Pity Peace and Love / Is God', it follows that when we pray, it is to these 'virtues of delight' that we address ourselves, as the first stanza explains, otherwise we would be foolishly or superstitiously making our devotions to something unknown.

All these things are propounded in the poem because the speaker is quite simply assured of the operation of the four divine virtues. It is quite possible, of course, to deny the divine virtues – expo-nents of selfism, the doctrine described at the beginning of this chapter and on pp. 85–7, always do – and we shall examine the consequences of denying them in the next poem we examine: *The Human Abstract* which is based on a selfist theory of man. This theory states that the 'virtues' are inculcated by fear or the desire to be well thought of, and it is not seldom, perhaps, that virtue, or a semblance of it, owes its being to such causes. But it should be pointed out that the selfist view is invariably held dogmatically. No selfist ever says, 'I behave well because I hope to gain by it, though there may be men who are altruistically virtuous.' All human behaviour must be comprehended in his theory. The speaker in *The Divine Image* has no theory – he is far too scientific for that. He observes the virtues and draws conclusions from what he observes, but he makes no attempt to explain them. No doubt the selfist expounds his theory because he does not find the virtues in himself, only selfish motives, but then it is semantically unsound to describe the behaviour that results in terms of the virtues, and it is scientifically unsound to assume that all human behaviour may be accounted for in terms of what he sees taking place in his own mind. The speaker in *The Divine Image* makes no assumptions about other men, as we shall see, and the conclusions he draws are true even if the divine virtues exist only in one man and for only a single instant.

The selfist categorizes all human motives and emotions. We have seen, for instance, how the mother in the experienced *A Cradle Song* (p. 63) knows all about the workings of her infant's mind because she equates it with her own. The virtues of 'Mercy Pity Peace and Love' enumerated in *The Divine Image* are not classes of feeling or behaviour at all, but are described as 'virtues of delight' (line 3). The implication is that they take their character from the person who displays them on the specific occasion of their display, and so they have infinite variety. The pleasures and pains of Experience are predictable and easily described, but delight is personal and inward: it stirs the whole being, is too complex and full for the person who experiences it to be able to 'put his finger on it', and carries him beyond the desire to define it. Also, although it is inward it is always associated with something beyond the self – we delight *in* something and the emotion never arises from mere acquisition. Here, delight arises from the exercise of 'Mercy Pity Peace and Love', all of which involve a movement of our feelings towards other persons and a desire for their good. In the context of the first stanza, the inwardness of the experience of the 'virtues of delight' is emphasized as well as their yearning – their set towards another:

> To Mercy Pity Peace and Love.
> All pray in their distress:
> And to these virtues of delight
> Return their thankfulness.

'Distress' and 'thankfulness' are very personal feelings, but here they emerge in prayer, in the attempt to communicate them to a larger Being. Blake makes his small words very expressive. Notice how prominently he places his 'to's', so as to emphasize the urgent outward movement of the mind at prayer – the 'setting towards' of thoughts and feelings longing to be made known.

In the third stanza, the four virtues are described, but in a way that emphasizes their fulness, variety, and liveliness. They are all modes of human energy, and together they compose the human being. No definition is offered because they manifest the being who displays them and the occasion on which he does so. They are not elements of behaviour, but aspects of it. They have no existence without each other and except as part of a complete activity, but we may conveniently distinguish them by their modes. 'Mercy has a human heart' because it is an inward disposition. We may feel it within ourselves and, in others, we may know of it because it manifests itself in the postures of the body and expressions of the countenance – manifests itself as 'Pity', which 'has a human face'. Pity is outward and discernible, like 'Peace, the human dress'. Peace exists between men and between nations, is a social manifestation of the inclinations of individuals. Like our clothing, it follows a fashion – the exact mode is learned, and may vary from time to time. But just as different fashions in clothing express an impulse to be decent in appearance, so our social habits show an impulse to be decent in our common behaviour, despite local differences in customs and tradition. The naked virtue is 'Love, the human form divine', and it is given most prominence in the poem, though Blake treats all four virtues together, altering the order in which he names them, or leaving one out, repeating them time after time as if sounding their harmony. 'Love' has 'the human form divine', because all the movements of the soul must come to a resolution in the states and actions of the body. Our being comes to expression only through the flesh, and all we may know of another is what his body, in some way, may show or do. We know of nothing that does not come to the body or from the body, and it is the focus of our universe.

Blake's separate enumeration of the virtues, and his association of them with the heart, face, form and dress, serves to distinguish them, but at the same time it shows that they may not be categorically separated, being modes, only, of the human. 'Mercy has a human heart', so it is a human being who knows the quality. 'Pity' has 'a human face', so it is a human being who displays the quality – and so on through the list. We know the virtues when we see them in deed or word, we may make general statements about virtuous behaviour, but their operation is too much a manifestation of the individual and of living circumstance for any easy formula or comprehensive definition to be possible, and the speaker does not attempt to provide any. Though he makes firm statements, he is not in the least doctrinaire or assertive.

As we have seen, the speaker does not attempt to describe as a part what is, in fact, a whole, and the virtues are not hypostatized components of man, but manifestations of living men. He makes no attempt to explain anything he cannot be quite sure of or describe anything he cannot see, and consequently his assertions about the human being are extremely moderate. He states that:

> all must love the human form.
> In heathen, turk or jew.

The implication of these lines is not that all men are basically the same. Perhaps they are, and God certainly dwells in them, as the virtues do, but the point is that the speaker knows nothing about any other man, whether he be fellow countryman or foreigner, except through his face, form and dress. He makes no statement about what lies within, for every man's soul is secret, and the speaker has no inclination to probe the secret, just as the mother in the innocent *A Cradle Song* had no desire to know what lay within her baby. All men are alien (not only those who are 'heathen, turk or jew'), all men are to be respected, and their privacy is to be respected too. Men's hearts may go out to one another, but they cannot plumb the depths of one another's souls. The speaker makes very confident statements about man:

> To Mercy Pity Peace and Love.
> All pray

and:

> Mercy Pity Peace and Love,
> Is man

but he may be firm because he offers the virtues as movements of the spirit, not as constituent factors in a psychology.

Each man is accorded his own privacy and dignity, and the speaker is not tempted to mass humanity together in an attempt to explain it. God, too, is allowed his secrecy, so that though the speaker knows what God displays he does not merge God and man:

> Mercy Pity Peace and Love.
> Is God . . .

An identical statement is made about man, but the statements are carefully separated in the second stanza. There is to be no confusion here, and though we know God by the divine virtues, we know no more. The careful division of the stanza in two parts makes it impossible to identify God and man, but at the same time it emphasizes the longing God has for man and that man has for God. The virtues of delight are all inward and they all yearn towards another. God is independently described, but is named as 'God our father dear' – named in the capacity in which man is drawn to him. And man, when he has been separately referred to, is seen in the capacity to which God is attracted – seen as 'Man his child and care'. The connexion, established through the virtues, is one of desire for the other, solicitude, gratitude, and thanksgiving.

The Divine Image is written in general terms – the virtues are not exemplified – but despite its theoretical style, there is no attempt to simplify what is observed, or to provide any final explanation. The four virtues are not tendencies in man, innate or acquired, which incline him to do well, but they *are* man who does well. The speaker does not undertake the task of the moral philosopher, who looks for factors influencing human behaviour, and who, therefore, dissects the mind and its motives. Such a dissection has its proper place, but is necessarily a dissection of the experienced, not the innocent mind, though it usually presents its findings as being true of all minds. A dogmatic approach of this sort is illustrated by Blake in *The Human Abstract* of the *Songs of Experience*, where the speaker discusses motives, not manifestations, though he uses the terms we have been examining: 'Mercy', 'Pity', 'Peace' and 'Love'. His conception of these qualities forms a striking contrast to that depicted in *The Divine Image*.

THE HUMAN ABSTRACT

Pity would be no more,
If we did not make somebody Poor;
And Mercy no more could be,
If all were as happy as we;

And mutual fear brings peace;   5
Till the selfish loves increase.
Then Cruelty knits a snare.
And spreads his baits with care.

He sits down with holy fears.
And waters the ground with tears;   10
Then Humility takes its root
Underneath his foot.

Soon spreads the dismal shade
Of Mystery over his head:
And the Catterpiller and Fly.   15
Feeds on the Mystery.

> And it bears the fruit of Deceit.
> Ruddy and sweet to eat:
> And the Raven his nest has made
> In its thickest shade.   20

> The Gods of the earth and sea.
> Sought thro' Nature to find this Tree
> But their search was all in vain:
> There grows one in the Human Brain

The poem is divided into three sections. Lines 1 – 4 are spoken by Blake's persona, lines 5 and 6 are also spoken by him, but with an undercurrent of irony added by Blake, and the remainder of the poem is an attack, by Blake, on the assumptions made by his imagined speaker (his persona) and the consequences of his thinking. The speaker asserts the selfist doctrine of human nature, so that, though he names the four virtues ('Pity', 'Mercy', 'peace' and 'love') in the six lines he speaks, he conceives them as a rationalist would, not as the 'virtues of delight'. The lines have a rather trite expected rhythm, because the view he puts forward is a stereotyped one, while the remainder of the poem has an irregular rhythm to accord with its harsh tone. On a first reading, the opening stanza seems quite reasonable:

> Mercy no more could be
> If all were as happy as we . . .

It cannot be denied that it requires the existence of misery for Mercy to be shown. If all men were prosperous and happy, there would be no occasion on which charity could be exercised, so, given the inevitable existence of unhappiness and poverty, these conditions do, at least, have the effect of eliciting the impulses which relieve them. The matter is more complex than this, however:

> Pity would be no more,
> If we did not make somebody Poor . . .

The conditions under which we live make it certain that in

providing for our own wants and the wants of our family we deprive others and perpetuate a state of society in which some persons are unfortunately placed. This condition persists, whether we like it or not, but it, too, has the effect of giving scope for Pity. There are not enough good things to go round to all the inhabitants of earth, and those who secure them place them beyond the reach of others, but that creates the circumstance in which charity may be shown. These truisms are so well worn that one distrusts the speaker who states them, and one distrusts the manner in which they are stated. Does he make the statements in order to emphasize the need for Pity and Mercy or is it his object to justify the existence of poverty and unhappiness? Clearly, he is not saying: 'Unhappiness exists and so we must show mercy' but: 'We accept the fact of unhappiness', and adds a very lame justification for the state of affairs. The speaker is uneasy, and he is attempting to reassure himself or to convince himself that he may take as much for himself as he can get and need not be very solicitous for those he deprives. It is a commonly held idea that competition is necessary to the health of societies, which cannot thrive unless men are obliged to give of their best in outdoing others. It can be argued, for instance, that a certain level of unemployment is desirable as it compels those who have employment to do their utmost to retain it, while if the level is not too high employers will be obliged to do their utmost to attract good workers. The argument may be turned many ways and there is, no doubt, much truth in it for the economist, but the speaker is using social and economic theory, not in its legitimate sphere, but in order to construct a personal morality which allows him to be more ruthless and more indifferent to the sufferings of others than a sensitive conscience would permit. He puts things upside down. The economist describes how things work out, despite man's better impulses, but the speaker attempts to regulate his impulses according to how he supposes they might work out. In short, he attempts to abolish conscience and lulls it with the notion that, as he is obliged to 'make somebody poor', he need not make much effort to avoid doing so. Also, he may be complacent about the fact that not all are 'as happy as we'.

The selfist idea is given clear statement at the beginning of the second stanza, though it is expressed in Blake's own bald words:

> And mutual fear brings peace;
> Till the selfish loves increase.

We are referred to a doctrine that was as well known in Blake's day as it is now, though it is usually stated in terms that make it sound more pleasing. The twentieth-century psychologist might speak of the 'self-regarding sentiment', and argue that this 'drive', together with others, helps fashion the socially acceptable person. Pope, echoing earlier thinkers, speaks, not of 'selfish loves', but of 'self-love', using the loftier term because, under the proper guidance of reason, so he argues, the passion becomes the source of our virtues:

> So drives self-love through just and through unjust,
> To one man's power, ambition, lucre, lust:
> The same self-love, in all, becomes the cause
> Of what restrains him, government and laws.
> . . . .
> How shall he keep, what, sleeping or awake,
> A weaker may surprise, a stronger take?
> His safety must his liberty restrain:
> All join to guard what each desires to gain.
> Forced into virtue thus, by self-defence,
> Even Kings learn'd justice and benevolence:
> Self-love forsook the path it first pursued,
> And found the private in the public good.
>   (*Essay on Man* III. 269)

The argument is a well-known one. Self-love inclines us to get what we can for ourselves – inclines us to 'power, ambition, lucre, lust' – but reason tells us that a condition of society in which these appetites were under no restraint would make us vulnerable; unable to defend ourselves from theft and violence.

We see, then, that our interest is best served by submitting our appetites to the control of laws and conventions, for though we cannot, under their confinement, seize upon whatever we desire, we ensure possession of what we can peaceably get. The foundation of peaceful societies, then, is the fear one man has for another, so that we are prepared to give up our freedom to do exactly what we like, and submit to control by institutions which will impose the same control on our fellow men. As Blake puts it: 'mutual fear brings peace', though he puts it bleakly and without enthusiasm, in contrast to Pope, who is sometimes enraptured at the idea of self-love 'push'd to social, to divine':

> Self-love but serves the virtuous mind to wake,
> As the small pebble stirs the peaceful lake;
> The centre moved, a circle straight succeeds,
> Another still, and still another spreads;
> Friend, parent, neighbour, first it will embrace;
> His country next; and next all human race;
> Wide and more wide, the o'erflowings of the mind
> Take every creature in, of every kind;
> Earth smiles around, with boundless bounty blest,
> And Heaven beholds its image in his breast.
>
> (*Essay on Man* IV. 363)

Pope's view is an optimistic one, and he takes great satisfaction in contemplating the wide overflowings of benevolence, leading to the pleasant condition of earth 'with boundless bounty blest'. Blake, who by now has taken the statement of his poem into his own hands, refers scathingly to 'the selfish loves increase', before going on, in the lines that follow, to state the consequence of the selfist philosophy as he sees it – not an earthly paradise, but a universal condition of self-deceit and hypocrisy.

Blake does not, in this poem or elsewhere, deny the truth of the rationalist doctrine he examines in the poem. On the contrary, it is only too true for too many men, and this is why it finds expression in the *Songs of Experience*. If any man, wanting to find the mainspring of human action, examines his own soul and finds a sufficient explanation in fear and selfishness, then who can contradict him? Only he knows what takes place in that realm, so his account is probably true – of himself. Probably true, not certainly true. Experience knows itself imperfectly, and often substitutes an idea of the self for what may in fact be there. The selfist doctrine is an over-simplification at best, and that increases the suspicion that it may be a theory imposed on the mind when it is examined, rather than an accurate account of what is revealed by dispassionate research. The chief danger of the doctrine is precisely that it is a doctrine, and so easily accepted and acted upon by persons who should know themselves better. It can stultify our better impulses, assist us in giving way to our worst impulses and, because it is dogmatic, cause our intelligence of ourselves and of others to diminish. The speaker in *The Human Abstract* has lied to himself, has tried to make himself comfortable about poverty and misery by rehearsing the rationalist theory of society – the idea that self-interest makes the world go round – and having started with a lie it is unlikely that he can get himself straight afterwards. He must add lies and perversions to his thinking until his mind becomes a thicket of deceits, and in the remainder of the poem Blake describes the vegetable growth of a forest of tangled distortions. His illustration to the poem depicts an old man in such a thicket, crouched beneath a net of his own mental contrivance from which he cannot escape.

The most noticeable feature of the self-deception which results in the growth of the tree of 'Mystery' and 'Deceit' is its false 'Humility' – indeed it is the seed from which the tree springs. The speaker submitted himself hypocritically, in the first six lines, to something larger than himself – submitted to social necessities, as he conceived them, and made a virtue, even, of self-interest. He was determined to achieve the impossible – to be, if selfish, then altruistically selfish for the good of all men. The moral of the poem is that we would do well to suspect men whose 'Humility' is such that they overlook doing good 'in minute particulars' (as Blake puts it elsewhere) and prefer 'holier' causes which benefit mankind or society, or which further God's will, or the will of the nation, or the plan of the universe. Dedication of this sort seems rather self-centred and does not take the needs or feelings of others into account:

> He sits down with holy fears.
> And waters the ground with tears . . .

As the word 'fears' indicates, this 'holy' act is superstitious – a bowing down to a self-made idol, not a reverence to a true light. The 'tears' which blind the downcast eyes of the idolater are hypocritical, shed in fear and self-pity, and make it impossible for him to see any interest but his own. There certainly are men who patiently labour for the good of humanity in general and do so with real humility, but they are usually men capable of particular good as well. The cause of general good is very often the cause of the bigot, the demagogue, the pedant, the hypocrite, the fool, and the scoundrel, and it is only too easy to give rein to a capacity for 'Cruelty' in the name of some 'holy' mission. Any history, with its account of crusades, inquisitions, pogroms, military interventions and so on, will provide confirmation, and confirm, also, the 'holy fears', 'Humility', and the excellence of the intentions of those who inaugurate and support these acts of public 'benefit'.

Any programme for mankind, whether it is based on the will of God, the will of the people, on social or economic theory, on an -ology or an -ism, is abstract by nature, and so capable of distortion and misuse. Even schemes and institutions which have great promise, being decently and benevolently conceived, based on intelligent thought and the examination of man's needs, may become the tools of the fanatic and the egotist. Rationalist schemes that are based on the principle of selfishness give those who subscribe to them every excuse for being egotistical and are just as liable as other theories, religious and political, to be dogmatically held. In the fourth stanza Blake likens the development of dogma to the spreading of a tree or a thicket. Light is progressively cut out as the tangles of theoretical elaboration spread, covering patches where the reasoning is thin, closing gaps through which alternative ideas might be seen, ramifying and elaborating so that all things may be comprehended within its 'shade'. As it spreads, the 'mysteries' of its being provide food for religious 'catterpillers' and political 'flies' – scholars, preachers and journalists, who explain what should be thought by the orthodox, expose what is heretical or deviant, provide commentaries for the erudite and articles of belief for the unlettered. Eventually, all who live beneath the tree take their mental sustenance from it, eating the 'fruit of Deceit', supposing that it alone is wholesome, living on a decaying tradition, just as the 'Raven' lives on carrion.

Blake's attack on dogmatism is scathing and extreme. He over-looks the fact that there are degrees of decency within orthodoxies as well as degrees between them, but his satire is contemptuous because he is more particularly concerned with the rationalist orthodoxy of the eighteenth century, which he regards as perni-cious. In the last stanza of the poem, however, the manner of the attack is relieved, though not rendered less scathing, by a touch of bleak humour. Selfist philosophies of the Enlightenment were said, by their advocates, to be 'natural', because they were derived simply from observation of the world about us, and reasonable deduction from what can be so observed. For most rationalists, the simplest explanation of human behaviour was based on the observation of man's fear and selfishness, and we have seen how Blake shows the inadequacy of the explanation by applying rational methods to a different set of observations in *On Anothers Sorrow* and *The Divine Image*. Observation, apparently, is not as straightforward and infallible a method as the 'natural philo-sophers' suppose it is, because the world reveals itself differently to different observers. The better rationalist philosophers were aware of this, though they often write as if they were not. The amateur philosopher of the time, the popularizer, and the layman were distinctly not aware, and appealed to 'Nature' as to an infallible authority, misusing it in the same way that Scripture may be misused to assert the 'truths' that suit the individual. In the last stanza of the song, we find the 'Gods of the earth and sea', who are nature gods, searching through their own realm to find the tree described in the poem (what object is more natural than a tree?) because they have so often heard the term 'natural' applied to it. They have heard Pope, for instance, declare that:

> God and Nature link'd the general frame,
> And bade self-love and social be the same.
>
> (*Essay on Man* III. 317)

But their search is 'all in vain'. Quite simply the tree isn't there – it is not a real thing, though the selfists attempt to give their argument authority by pointing to it as though it were. Like any other doctrine, the selfist doctrine is produced 'in the Human Brain' where the Gods finally discover it, to Blake's grim amusement. The dogma postulated in the first six lines of the poem is abstract, interpretative, and no more substantially true than other products of the mind.

The title of the song tells us that the tree is 'abstract', a growth 'in the Human Brain', though the word 'abstract' here is ambiguous, and copies the dual nature of the poem. In the body of the song Blake talks with two voices – first that of his persona, though we detect the contempt with which Blake presents him, then, after the first six lines, the poet breaks in entirely in his own withering tones. The title tells us that the poem is a 'human abstract' because Blake's persona supposes that he presents an epitome of what is to be found in the nature of man, but the alternative meaning of 'abstract' informs us that the epitome is merely conceptual, and so adds Blake's comment to the statement of his speaker.

The Human Abstract is the counterpart in experienced songs of *The Divine Image*. Both poems discuss the four virtues, though they are known differently in each. The innocent speaker shows that they are characterized by delight and yearning towards another, that they express complex movements of the soul in complex situations, and that they are of infinite variety, but he makes no attempt to define their origin. The experienced speaker, who thinks in terms of motives, explains the virtues and all other human behaviour as the result of self-love, which gives him a simple formula for his psychological and social thinking, but the formula has to sustain a cumbersome weight of rationalizations if it is to be made to fit everywhere. The innocent speaker includes God in his view of the virtues, though he does not attempt any metaphysical speculation, and is content simply to be aware of the manifestations of God which he finds presented to his attention. The experienced speaker does not mention God at all because, being a rationalist, determined to explain everything 'naturally', he is obliged to banish the supernatural from his system. Not that all rationalists are atheists, but it follows from their method that unpredictable forces must be set at a comfortable remove, and God is confined to heaven where he cannot interfere in human affairs. He was responsible, a great while ago, for ordering the system of the universe, establishing its laws so that all works out for the best ultimately, but leaving it, thereafter, to run itself. In the next chapter we shall examine some of the experienced ideas of a universe run without an active God or without any God at all, and see some of the ways in which the tree of 'natural' explanation ramifies into 'Mystery' and superstition.

5

CONTRARY IDEAS OF GOD

In the state of Experience God is thought of as a mysterious Being, though he may be known indirectly through the operation of his laws. In *The Tyger*, for instance, he is inscrutable, and Earth, in *Earth's Answer*, sees him as 'Starry Jealousy', the tyrant who binds the world to his will. There are other ways in which he is conceived, always as remote, usually with the qualities of experienced man, always powerful, and so to blame for the pains and unpleasantnesses of earthly life. These ideas are best suited to Experience which does not recognize the divine virtues and so needs, or supposes it needs, an arbitrary and terrifying lawmaker and judge to enforce decent behaviour. Innocence knows of God more intimately, though it does not pretend to know all about him and has no wish to know him fully. God is not necessarily seen as all powerful, and he is not associated with the end of life and time, but is present in both and his importance is due to his presence. Innocence does not think much about heaven and the after-life, and in the innocent religious poems we have examined – *The Lamb*, *On Anothers Sorrow* and *The Divine Image* – there is no mention of eternity. Even when heaven is described, as in *The Little Black Boy*, it is thought of as a place to which we go in order to continue to enjoy the energies of life, and continue the obligations we enjoy fulfilling here. It is never a place of reward for good behaviour.

The Little Black Boy

My mother bore me in the southern wild,
And I am black, but O! my soul is white.
White as an angel is the English child:
But I am black as if bereav'd of light.

My mother taught me underneath a tree   5
And sitting down before the heat of day.
She took me on her lap and kissed me.
And pointing to the east began to say.

Look at the rising sun: there God does live
And gives his light. and gives his heat away.   10
And flowers and trees and beasts and men receive
Comfort in morning joy in the noon day.

And we put on earth a little space.
That we may learn to bear the beams of love.
And these black bodies and this sun-burnt face   15
Is but a cloud, and like a shady grove.

For when our souls have learn'd the heat to bear
The cloud will vanish we shall hear his voice.
Saying: come out from the grove my love & care.
And round my golden tent like lambs rejoice.   20

Thus did my mother say and kissed me.
And thus I say to little English boy.
When I from black and he from white cloud free.
And round the tent of God like lambs we joy:

Ill shade him from the heat till he can bear.   25
To lean in joy upon our fathers knee.
And then Ill stand and stroke his silver hair.
And be like him and he will then love me.

Blake added two illustrations to this song. At the head of the
poem we are shown the little boy with his mother, seated beneath
their tree. He has been listening to her, and now points upwards
to heaven as if he understands that the 'golden tent' of God is
there. The sun is seen just above the horizon. An illustration at
the end of the poem shows the little black boy and the white boy
at the knee of God who is depicted as Christ the Shepherd. This
second illustration invites us to include the Christian tradition in
our reading, though the poem is not exclusively Christian. The
Songs of Innocence are never committed to any specific doctrine –

'heathen, turk, or jew' may show the virtues of delight, and God
'dwells' with the virtues, not in institutions. *The Little Black Boy*
is part heathen in its references, and the child is told to 'Look
on the rising sun: there God does live'. Also, there are references
to the Song of Solomon, pagan in its tone, in 'I am black, but
. . .', and 'come out of the grove, my love & care'. Innocence
fructifies whatever religious notions come its way, while the same
notions may be blighted by Experience, and we have seen the
Christian myth and Christian morality differently used in each of
The Chimney Sweeper songs. *The Little Black Boy* is, however, the
most pointedly Christian of the *Songs of Innocence* as it centres on
the idea of the resurrection of the dead and an after-life in heaven.
Although he appears in the illustration, Christ is not named in the
poem – he never is in the *Songs of Innocence*, though we may take
some of the poems as referring to Christ if we wish. This poem
talks, simply, of God, who is also very sparingly named by
innocent speakers.

The little black boy accepts his life as a gift from God; he takes
it gratefully just as it is given and uses it to good purpose, though
that life is anything but an easy one. He is probably a slave,
regarded by his overseer as one 'bereav'd of light' – a beast of
burden destined for an existence of ceaseless toil and harsh
punishment. It is no wonder that he cannot refer to God's gift
simply as a delightful one. The 'light' and the 'heat' are received
by 'flowers and trees and beasts and men' as 'Comfort in morning
joy in the noon day' (line 12), but the 'beams of love' are also
something that he must 'learn to bear' (line 14). He is thankful for
his life, but knows only too well that it is a hard one. His circumstances are painful, but it does not occur to him to wonder why
they are not different or to reproach the Creator for what they are.
Innocence, as has been remarked, fructifies what is given to it,
and he takes the lesson taught him by his mother as a guide to
living fully and with understanding. She tells him of the death of
the body and resurrection in heaven, saying that the body 'Is but
a cloud, and like a shady grove' which we leave when we die, so
that we may 'rejoice' round the 'golden tent' of God. There is no
hint in what she says that heaven is a compensation for the pains

of life, and the period in the shade of the grove is one in which the beams of God's love are felt – a time of necessary preparation for the fuller light of heaven. The same warmth is felt on earth as in heaven, and it cannot be borne in heaven if one has not acclimatized to it on earth. The warmth is the heat of love, and the black boy listens to his mother, following her advice to exercise love while in the 'shady grove'. What is heaven, after all, but a place where love is known? – and how wise to anticipate the 'joy' of heaven here and now. The 'little English boy', who has not anticipated the heat of love, has to learn to bear it when he gets there, unlike the black boy who arrives in a fit condition. He is better prepared because he feels compassion for the white child who regards him with disdain. He has been more fortunate, perhaps, than the white child in having more to bear on earth, and so a greater opportunity to show tolerance and kind response. There is, of course, nothing self-congratulatory in the black boy's comparison of himself with the white boy in heaven. He merely regards himself as being blessed in his adverse circumstances, which have given him an opportunity to love. The white boy has been less blessed, so he will have to be assisted when they come to 'the tent of God', and the black boy will help him there to know the love he has missed. No doubt it will be easier when the black boy is 'like him', and the black and white 'clouds' are gone, but this is not meant as a reproach. The black boy certainly does not regard his present advantage – his opportunity to show charity – as an entitlement to enter heaven. Both boys arrive there eventually, but the present advantage of the black boy will enable him to continue the advantage in the next life. Heaven is a place where the responsibilities he enjoys now may be further exercised, and life on earth may be a time of knowing the joys of heaven. The 'cloud' and 'shady grove' of the body are grateful shelters which filter the glare of God's sun, and the agents which disclose him to us, not shrouds to be cast off with satisfaction.

Many of the *Songs of Innocence* are based on an intuition of the efficacy of sympathy, of care and charity, of love as a principle actively at work. There is no attempt to account for the principle or to attribute it to something else. Some of the poems are child-like, because children most readily respond to affection and give it spontaneously. They understand the simple description of God as 'our Father' – an idea that is by no means inferior to the elaborately abstract conceptions of the adult. The child often interprets the events of the natural world as indicating sympathy between dumb creatures, and even when confronted with pain and death sees these as compensated for elsewhere, even if only in heaven. The accuracy of these ideas, the correctness or otherwise of the conception of God, nature and heaven, is not important. They are all matters on which no certainty is possible – Experience, like Innocence, can offer only conjectures, and the conjectures, both in Innocence and Experience, are of interest chiefly as indications of the quality of the mind that underlies them. What the *Songs of Innocence* point to is the sweetness of the soul that can support a faith in the virtues of delight, applying the faith to fictions as well as to fact – to the tired myths and stories it inherits as well as to its own discoveries about the world. The myths become real enough in any way that matters if the soul that entertains them can provide the body and truth of its own affections. The 'fictions' of Innocence, indeed, possess more substance than many of the 'facts' of Experience, and the innocent persona is surprisingly clear-minded, even when he is very young.

Not all Blake's innocents are children, but many are, probably because children have a better chance of displaying Innocence than the adult, to whom moments of spontaneity come infrequently. The little black boy is a child and he believes what his mother tells him about heaven. The literal truth of her account (myth, fiction or fact) is irrelevant to Blake, who is interested in the substantial truth of the existence in mother and child of the virtues of delight. Other innocent speakers put forward notions about love in God, peace in nature, and pity in heaven that may be designated child-like, though this merely means that, though the ideas cannot be proved (or disproved), they are asserted with the simple confidence of one whose innate charity inclines him to find the ideas credible and significant. The myth becomes established on a reality which confers truth upon it. In the song *Night*, for instance, it is asserted that there is divine care for all creatures, and an eternal life awaits each of them. Most of the *Songs of Innocence* show a sense of there being benign influences at work in the world without identifying them exactly, but in *Night* they are personified as 'angels' who are 'unseen' but

> pour blessing.
> And joy without ceasing.
> On each bud and blossom.
> And each sleeping bosom.

These angels are not mentioned elsewhere in the innocent songs, though they are often seen in the illustrations to the text. They keep 'every beast' from harm, but we are told that:

> When wolves and tygers howl for prey
> They pitying stand and weep;
> Seeking to drive their thirst away,
> And keep them from the sheep.
> But if they rush dreadful:
> The angels most heedful.
> Recieve each mild spirit.
> New worlds to inherit.

The angels do everything in their power to protect and to comfort, but that power has its limits, and they cannot prevent the 'tyger' from devouring the lamb. What they can do is to 'recieve' the spirits of the dead in 'New worlds' where the lion cares for the sheep:

> 'And now beside thee, bleating lamb.
> I can lie down and sleep;
> Or think on him who bore thy name
> Grase after thee and weep.

Love is weak and it is strong. The angels are supernatural beings with some power in the world, but that power does not lie in 'control' as it is understood by Experience. The angels do not order things to be done or not done, but 'seek' to make their pity known. Love has nothing to do with imposing the will, only with allowing affection to be felt, and further interference would be unthinkable. Innocence never asks why God or the angels allow cruelty, death, or any other diminishment to take place, because it does not associate love with an exercise of authority or strength. That is an experienced concept of love. Innocence has, nevertheless, full confidence in the strength and efficacy of love, and that confidence is expressed in this poem by the innocent speaker's finding a place, even if only in 'New worlds', where it is ultimately triumphant, and the lion can say:

> wrath by his meekness
> And by his health. sickness.
> Is driven away.
> From our immortal day.

The gentle qualities of Jesus are realized for all, and 'wrath' and the cruelty of the world are its sicknesses. It follows that descriptions of the world as a place of competition, of selfishness, of the survival of the fittest, and other rationalist explanations, though they may be accurate, are for the innocent speaker descriptions only of its pathology, not of its healthy functioning.

The speaker of *Night* is, perhaps, a child, who expresses his religious ideas. The intuitions which support those innocent ideas may be seen also in the statements of the adult, not necessarily statements with a religious content. The description in *The Shepherd*, for instance, gives only slight hints that the poem is meant to be a religious one, yet the values affirmed are very similar to those we have just examined.

The Shepherd.

> How sweet is the Shepherds sweet lot,
> From the morn to the evening he strays:
> He shall follow his sheep all the day
> And his tongue shall be filled with praise.

For he hears the lambs innocent call.
And he hears the ewes tender reply.
He is watchful while they are in peace.
For they know when their Shepherd is nigh.

The shepherd in Blake's illustration is a sturdy man who stands
easily at a little distance from his flock, quietly overlooking the
sheep as they graze. His strength will never be required, as his
presence is sufficient to ensure their 'peace'. His rôle is, like that
of the angels in *Night*, a passive one, but his presence confers the
atmosphere necessary to the tranquillity of his flock, which, in
its dumb way, is aware of his 'control'. The 'control', however,
is of the innocent variety, which involves care, confers freedom,
and is not an imposition of will. Blake is quite clear on this point.
The shepherd does not guide his flock, but 'strays' with it, and
we are told that 'He shall follow his sheep all the day'. What is
'sweet' is his 'lot' – the life which is conferred upon him and
which he takes as it comes. He is as apparently passive in acceptance here as he is in his acceptance of the direction taken by his
flock, so the word 'lot' implies. But this passivity shows a
strength in the shepherd which gives comfort and is derived from
the comfort and confidence he feels. We are made very much
aware, as we read the poem, of the atmosphere of tolerance and
affection. It exists between the 'lamb' which 'calls' and the ewe
with its 'tender reply'; it is established, in another way, by the
watchful glance of the shepherd; and it is imparted to him too,
for his 'tongue' is 'filled with praise'. This is the only sure
indication in the poem that it has a religious dimension, and even
here we are not necessarily referred to the supernatural. Perhaps
the shepherd praises God by addressing formal prayers to him,
but his 'tongue' is 'filled with praise' whether he does so or not,
because any word he utters and any deed he performs is an
affirmation of his acceptance of his 'lot', of the ease of his mind
and demeanour, of the strength which allows him to act by con-
ceding. He gives freedom to his flock, and he is free himself, though
the freedom is of the innocent kind – it is not a licence to do just
what he pleases, but a willing inclination to do what is fitting.

99

In lines 3 and 4, which are written in the future, not the present tense, there is possibly another indication that the poem is a religious one. Perhaps we are meant to understand that the shepherd 'shall' follow his sheep and utter his praise in 'New worlds'. But if this is implied, the remainder of the poem makes it quite clear that he 'shall' do so because he performs these acts in the present world. Blake's interest is in the world we know, and the qualities of mind which make religions possible, rather than in any specific religious tenet. We are free to see the shepherd as Christ the Shepherd if we wish – the lack of specific reference to Christ does not set Christianity aside – but the purpose of the poem is to describe the human capacity for charity and tolerance which gives substance to much Christian thought. These capacities can provide a basis for other types of speculation as well.

The speculation in *A Dream* is of such a nature that very few adults could allow it to be valid, yet they would concede that the impulse behind the speculation gives the poem significance. The song is a quaint one, told by a child, in which an ant has lost its way at night and utters its distress:

> O my children! do they cry.
> Do they hear their father sigh.
> Now they look abroad to see,
> Now return and weep for me.

The observer drops a tear, but the glow-worm who acts as 'watchman of the night' tells the ant that:

> I am set to light the ground,
> While the beetle goes his round:
> Follows now the beetles hum,
> Little wanderer hie thee home.

The fantasy is founded on the secure conviction, held by the observer, that care of all creatures for one another, even down to the very smallest, is an effective and operative force in the world.

It tells us a great deal about the speaker. He is deeply concerned – so concerned that he imputes his feeling to the glow-worm and beetle, and he is sure that even the emmet in the midst of her distress thinks first of her husband and children, and knows that they have no thoughts but for her. The poem is interpretative, of course, but it is imaginatively, not dogmatically so, and contains an imagined truth. The mutual concern described in the poem implies the presence of a virtue in the speaker which needs no further proof of its existence than that it finds utterance in his 'Dream'.

In *A Dream* the innocent speaker, being young, has brought the divine virtues very much down to earth, and finds them exemplified in the activities of the insects. He probably lies in the grass, observes the struggles of an ant, and the story he tells forms itself in his mind, coming rather as a dream would. In other songs, divine figures are brought down to earth, like the angels in *Night*. In *The Little Boy Lost* and *The Little Boy Found* God appears to the child 'lost in the lonely fen', and rescues him, but can appear in no more wonderful form than that of the child's own father, and can do no more wonderful thing than restore him to his mother. To the child, the commonplace is sufficiently miraculous, and paternal affection sufficiently divine. The tendency in Experience, however, is to find the commonplace contemptible and human affections inadequate or distasteful, and this may be so even when there is a preoccupation with the divine, or with what Experience takes to be divine. Blake points this out in *To Tirzah* of the *Songs of Experience*.

To Tirzah

Whate'er is born of Mortal Birth,
Must be consumed with the Earth
To rise from Generation free:
Then what have I to do with thee?

The Sexes sprung From Shame & Pride
Blowd in the morn; in evening died

But Mercy changd Death into Sleep;
The Sexes rose to work & weep.

Thou Mother of my Mortal part
With cruelty didst mould my Heart
And with false self-decieving tears
Didst bind my Nostrils Eyes & Ears.

Didst close my Tongue in senseless clay
And me to Mortal Life betray:
The Death of Jesus set me free.
Then what have I to do with thee?

It is Raised a Spiritual Body.

Blake's illustration to the poem shows the naked figure of a man, apparently dead, being raised and supported by two women, while an old man prepares to pour the contents of a ewer over the body. On his clothing the last words of the poem are written: 'It is Raised a Spiritual Body.' These persons are grouped beneath an apple tree and the arrangement and general appearance of the figures is reminiscent of paintings depicting the body of Christ being prepared by the two Marys and Joseph of Arimathaea after it has been taken from the cross. The crucifixion is referred to in the poem, and the speaker has given his own interpretation to the event ('The Death of Jesus set me free'), though he is, apparently, echoing the teaching of St Paul, who says, when talking of the death of the body:

It is sown in corruption; it is raised
in incorruption:
It is sown in dishonour; it is
raised in glory: it is sown in weakness;
it is raised in power:
It is sown a natural body: it is
raised a spiritual body.

(I Corinthians 15. 42)

St Paul is explaining the resurrection, and commences this

section of his epistle: 'Now if Christ be preached that he rose from the dead, how say some among you that there is no resurrection of the dead?' He goes on to explain that all shall be 'made alive' in Christ, and concludes by answering the doubt: 'How are the dead raised up? and with what body to they come?' He explains that the 'earthly' body dies in order that the 'heavenly' body may live, just as the seed dies that a plant may live: 'There are also celestial bodies, and bodies terrestrial: but the glory of the celestial is one, and the glory of the terrestrial is another' (I Corinthians 15. 40).

St Paul gives his two bodies their due importance and he honours both of them. The speaker in *To Tirzah* dishonours his terrestrial body and has no proper conception of a celestial one. His question 'Then what have I to do with thee?' is addressed first to that part of him (for, unlike St Paul, he divides himself into two parts) which must be 'consumed with the Earth'. Then in the second half of the poem he directs the question to 'Thou Mother of my Mortal part' – to his human mother and to mother earth who brings all mortal life into being. He echoes Christ's words to his mother at Cana, but interprets the statement as a rejection of Christ's ties with the flesh, and a negation of the value of life on earth. He sees his soul as being, in some way, separate from his body and untouched by its doings, waiting only for the time when the encumbrance of the flesh shall be taken from him, and he will be 'free' in an eternal elysium. Life, for him, is 'senseless', it knows nothing of the celestial verities, and is a pointless interim spent in a prison of 'senseless clay'. Even his 'Nostrils Eyes & Ears', which take him beyond himself, are a confinement, limiting him to a knowledge of what is earthy and mortal. He looks forward to the time when he can 'rise from Generation free' and finds his present condition a contemptible one. The world and the flesh are fallen, are prisons where man can endure the alternative to the death sentence that was remitted after Adam and Eve had sinned:

> But Mercy changed Death into Sleep;
> The sexes rose to work & weep.

The speaker refers to the judgement passed by the Lord God, who said to Eve: 'I will greatly multiply thy sorrow and thy conception; in sorrow thou shalt bring forth children . . .', and to Adam: 'In the sweat of thy face shalt thou eat bread, till thou return unto the ground . . .'

In the second stanza, the fall of man is incorrectly associated, as it often is, with a sexual awakening: 'The Sexes sprung from Shame & Pride . . .' No doubt the speaker derives this from the biblical statement that Adam and Eve, after eating the fruit, knew that they were naked, but the notion springs, ultimately, from the fundamental dislike of all things of the flesh which permeates the poem. Every attempt is made to sanctify the dislike: Genesis is misused, St Paul is misunderstood, and the crucifixion is robbed of its proper significance for the convenience of the speaker. It is this last distortion that makes his statements especially unpleasant. An air of smug insensibility runs through the poem, but one could find it possible to pity the man who is so determined to deprive himself of any enjoyment of his present existence, and to deprive himself, if he but knew it, of all rights to a future life. Any pity one might have is turned to contempt, however, by the self-congratulatory tone of 'The Death of Jesus set me free'. The speaker has his guarantee of immortality, he has not had to do a thing for it, and it makes him feel very superior. To emphasize the conceited insensibility of the speaker, Blake shows, at the foot of the poem, the broken body of the man who did accept the flesh and whose agony is the source of the speaker's self-satisfaction. Even the agony felt by his mother at the time of his birth is treated with disdain, and her pangs are dismissed as the cause of 'false self-decieving tears'. She carries the sentence passed on Eve, and carries it in a world where nothing is significant, not even the pains that make people so acutely aware of themselves and of their mortal flesh. The speaker, who is probably as comfortable in body as he is in mind, allows himself to be indifferent to suffering and dwells on the wrong done to him when he was 'bound' and 'closed' in the body. He does not regard his life, even, as an avenue to immortality or as a probation for the after-life, but simply as a meaningless infliction to be endured. The little black boy, it might be remembered, who also believes in a hereafter, looks on life as a period when the heavenly virtues are to be enjoyed. It is not, for him, a period of waiting or of probation, but of fulfilment.

The fall of man and the redemption are both referred to in the course of the poem, and both these events are brought to mind by Blake's illustration. The tree shown is an apple-tree, and traditionally the apple is the forbidden fruit of the Garden of Eden. Beneath the tree lies the dead redeemer. The old man who anoints the body of Christ resembles the decrepit figure of Experience, frequently seen in Blake's illustrations. He has no intention of relinquishing his hold on life, unlike the young Christ before him who was prepared to make the sacrifice. The speaker of the poem rejects the life of the body, but he, too, has no intention of relinquishing his hold, and sees the after-life as a curious prolongation of the present – the natural body 'is Raised a Spiritual Body'. It is difficult to understand what is meant – bodies are physical, and the words 'Spiritual Body', as they are used here, seem to be contradictory. What is clear is that the speaker finds no value in life but is unwilling to leave it and visualizes his future state as being identical with his present condition, except that it is 'spiritual', and so not subject to decay. As he has never known satisfaction in the flesh, it is not surprising that he is unwilling to abandon the idea that he will obtain it, or something like it, and his notion of eternity is that of endless time spent in a body that is, somehow, not a body.

The title of the song, *To Tirzah*, refers, presumably, to the Song of Solomon: 'Thou art beautiful, O my love, as Tirzah, comely as Jerusalem' (4. 4). But the poem is written in defiance of the loving form of address and admiration of physical beauty found in that passionate song of praise. The speaker immediately disowns 'Generation' and goes on to reject the enjoyment of the body and to express his contempt of its sexual aspect. If he could accept the Song of Solomon at all, it would be in the spiritual and allegorical meaning attributed to the poem, but he seems to have perceived that it cannot be taken exclusively in that way, and is best rejected outright. It would be wisest, from his point of view, to have nothing to do with the deceptive allurements of the physical, even if they are only referred to in order to describe, figuratively, the marriage of Christ and the Church.

In *To Tirzah*, Blake presents a speaker whose religion is founded on superstitions and irrational beliefs, and as the beliefs are unreasonable, they are held dogmatically. God is a supernatural figure who exists in the land to which the Sun-flower hopes to travel, but, by his sacrifice of himself, he has so arranged things that the bodiless bodies of men shall join him there. Because Adam disobeyed his commands he punishes us with the world we live in, but he has also redeemed us to eternal life. The speaker accepts all this without question, presumably because it suits him to do so; his interpretation is crude, and his beliefs are vulgar, but we have seen the innocent mind take equally crude beliefs, obviously from a vulgar source, and transmute them into a faith that is neither superstitious nor irresponsible. The experienced speaker of *To Tirzah* would regard himself as a more sophisticated thinker than the little black boy or the innocent chimney sweep, but it is an anomaly shown by Blake that Experience, though it controls our world and runs our institutions, often does so in crudity and ignorance, not in subtlety and wisdom. Innocence is weak in the worldly sense, and usually inarticulate when confronted by the assertions of Experience, but its knowledge is basically stronger, so that, though Innocence is put down time after time, its intuitions are re-asserted, to the benefit of mankind. The brassy rationalism of *The Human Abstract*, for instance, denies the existence of a disinterested sympathy in man, and transforms the four virtues into social accomplishments. The speaker in *The Divine Image* looks into his soul and, finding the virtues there, quietly and rationally reinstates them.

In some of the songs, Innocence and Experience confront each other, and the result is that Innocence is destroyed, as in *A Little Girl Lost*, or that the innocent statements are overlooked, as the words of the Bard are overlooked by Earth. In *A Little Boy Lost* the priest goes more directly to work and, because the boy acts as a reproach to him and all he stands for, puts the offender to death.

A Little BOY Lost

Nought loves another as itself
Nor venerates another so.
Nor is it possible to thought
A greater than itself to know:

And Father how can I love you,
Or any of my brothers more?
I love you like the little bird
That picks up crumbs around the door.

The Priest sat by and heard the child.
In trembling zeal he siez'd his hair:
He led him by his little coat:
And all admir'd the Priestly care.

And standing on the altar high.
Lo what a fiend is here! said he:
One who sets reason up for judge
Of our most holy Mystery.

The weeping child could not be heard.
The weeping parents wept in vain:
They strip'd him to his little shirt.
And bound him in an iron chain.

And burn'd him in a holy place.
Where many had been burn'd before:
The weeping parents wept in vain.
Are such things done on Albions shore.

Blake ends his poem with a ridiculous question. We all know that such things are not done in England, though we are convinced that atrocities are committed on foreign shores. The burning of the boy is grotesque, but the conclusion heightens the preposterous nature of the incidents which lead up to it. Those incidents are only too reminiscent of what really happens at home, and we all know that there are less drastic but effective ways of dealing with little boys who ask awkward questions. The poem is made ridiculous in order to caricature absurdities we know well.

It is absurd, for instance, that the priest should condemn the child for taking his own priestly rationale to its logical extreme, and it is absurd that the boy and his parents should be so bewildered and feel so guilty when he is punished.

The statement made by the child in the first two stanzas is, apparently, a rationalistic one similar to that made at the opening of *The Human Abstract* (pp. 82–91). It asserts that man is self-centred, and places 'realistic' limits on the love he can give. The first two lines remind us of Pope's:

> God loves from whole to parts: but human soul
> Must rise from individual to the whole.
> Self-love but serves the virtuous mind to wake,
> As the small pebble stirs the peaceful lake. . . .
>
> (*Essay on Man* IV. 361)

The child has heard some version of the selfist doctrine, has applied it to what the priest has taught him, and finds a contradiction between the rationalist truism and the religious injunction. The priest has expounded the two commandments: 'Thou shalt love the Lord thy God with all thy heart, and with all thy soul, and with all thy mind . . . Thou shalt love thy neighbour as thyself.' These laws, which are straightforward enough in themselves, have become, in the hands of the Christian priest, just what they became in the days of the scribes and Pharisees: 'heavy burdens and grievous to be borne.' The priest has delivered many sermons linking love with God, with sin, with faith, with the sacraments, with proper observance. 'Love' is a part of his mystique, now so refined and ingenious that, in the name of love, he is prepared to torture and kill. He certainly feels justified in burning the little boy who finds the commandments unrealistic and questions them:

> Nought loves another as itself
> Nor venerates another so.

The child puts his doubts to God the Father while at prayer, for he has reduced God to simple terms he can understand. The Priest, sitting watchfully by, has overheard the prayer, and seizes his victim.

The little boy has tried to look at love in a reasonable and practical way. That is bad enough – he innocently sets himself up in opposition to the expert – but he does worse in suggesting that the expert has no right to any authority at all – that the mystery he professes to teach is beyond the powers of normal human comprehension:

> Nor is it possible to thought
> A greater than itself to know:

This is also a part of rationalist doctrine. Pope, for instance, states that our ignorance in respect of God's designs is comparable to that of the horse or the ox in respect of our own purposes:

> When the proud steed shall know why man restrains
> His fiery course, or drives him o'er the plains;
> When the dull ox, why now he breaks the clod,
> Is now a victim, and now Egypt's god:
> Then shall man's pride and dulness comprehend
> His actions', passions', beings' use and end
>> (*Essay on Man* I. 61)

The little boy gives his version of this in addressing his heavenly Father:

> I love you like the little bird
> That picks up crumbs around the door.

The priest sees the implication – the statement brings his mystery into disrepute. Only those to whom direct revelation is given are entitled to make confident statements about the divine purpose. Others must trust what they are told, and must give some reason for their acceptance. It is sufficient for a child to cite his authority, for his trust is an act of love which is reason enough. It is sufficient for the innocent to demonstrate, in giving his reasons, the existence of the divine virtues which lend colour to religious faith. The priest, however, not being a good one, and being without humility towards his mystery, would like to be believed simply on his insistence, for his belief, whatever origins it may have had, has become a personal possession, and his stock-in-trade. It is significant that in judging the child he places himself 'on the altar high'. What he expounds is an ecclesiolatry, not a faith. It is without reverence or hesitation before the unknown, but dogmatically insists on an absolute knowledge vested in himself. Ironically, the words of the boy exactly describe the position taken by the priest whose word is to be the final authority, and whose thought, therefore, knows no 'greater than itself'. But then, he wants his words and thoughts to be taken as being, somehow, divine.

There is a further irony or absurdity in the fact that Blake, himself, could hardly approve of the rationalist clichés on which the boy's statements are based, and yet he shows the child as innocent enough, and shows how he transforms these truisms. It is not possible for thought 'A greater than itself to know', but it is not essential to thought that it should be selfish and self-protective as the rationalist assumes it is. Also it is not necessary for thought to know a 'greater than itself' in order that it should know the divine, provided that thought is informed by the divine virtues, as the *Songs of Innocence* imply throughout. Indeed, there is no other way of enjoying God's presence than by recognizing and exercising Mercy, Love, Pity and Peace. The boy tells his heavenly Father that he loves him 'like the little bird', and seems, like Pope, to be stressing man's inability to comprehend God's purposes. That is what the priest assumes him to mean, and takes it as a personal affront and as a heresy. The heresy would be seen as an even worse one if the priest could detect a further implication in the child's words. Pope states that our knowledge is very limited, and we must be content to accept our limitations in the corner of the universe allotted to us, while being aware that there is 'a greater' than the human somewhere. The boy denies, even, that thought may recognize the existence of this unknown greater realm, and his metaphor of the 'little bird' suggests that the universe, for man, is sufficiently contained in man. Not only is the bird unable to conceive the purpose of the man who put out the crumbs, but it does not attempt to do so, and in picking up the crumbs it makes a complete acknowledgement of the man in a manner appropriate to a bird. The bird gives its form of thanks simply in accepting the crumbs, and the child gives proper love to God in simply accepting his creation spontaneously. The priest, who knows no spontaneity, knows nothing of the creation and very little of God, though he gives formal thanks to a Creator of his own mental construction.

He could do no otherwise – men are obliged to theorize about God – but he has called on God from the worst elements in his nature, and we sense the divine only in our best inclinations. Religions have their source in divine revelation, but must be continued by tradition, speculation and exposition, all processes of 'thought'. The priest is angered when the boy 'sets reason up for judge / Of our most holy Mystery', not because the boy describes a process repugnant to priestcraft but threatens to 'give the game away' by describing one essential to it. It reduces the priest's knowledge to an ordinary human sort by exposing the pretence that he has private sources of information. No wonder he is alarmed. Religions do receive another impetus than tradition and ratiocination, of course, or they would soon become historical curiosities. We must look to our own natures to see, if we can, what is revealed of the divine there, and incorporate it in our thought, so confirming what we are told – but that innocent insight is not known to the priest described in the song.

The last four stanzas of the poem are grimly derisive. The sense of duty and triumph in the priest are made ridiculous by the pathetic 'little coat' which he seizes in 'trembling zeal', and the dutiful and sadistic breaking of the butterfly by admiring followers is grotesquely contrasted with the weeping of the victim. The child cannot be heard, though presumably he would like to explain that he had not meant to be offensive, and the parents weep 'in vain', partly because they are helpless to prevent the proceedings and partly because they are helpless to save the child by justifying him. The doctrine of love has prevailed over human compassion and parental affection, as Blake explains in *The Human*

Abstract, where 'humility' and dogma sanctified as 'mystery' permit 'cruelty' to knit its snare. The proceedings described by Blake are absurd, but their resemblance to absurdities that take place daily is too close for amusement to enter our response.

For the little black boy, life may be often painful, but it is never trivial. The speaker in *To Tirzah* turns away from life with contempt and the priest, who holds life cheap, thinks only of his 'Mystery' which is beyond human experience. The priest punishes the child for his rationalist heresy, but the rationalist, too, sets God beyond place and beyond time so that he may give an understandable and full account of the world in terms of determinate factors. So that there may be no mystery about his description of things and so that he may be in control of himself and in apparent control of his circumstances, he places God in a remote sphere where he may be ignored, though devotional gestures may be made towards him. Rationalism (deism) leads, ultimately, to agnosticism and atheism because once God has been seen as ineffectual the next step is to see that he is unimportant or negligible. The effect of the priest's variety of religion is very similar – God is a distant and incomprehensible figure, though it is possible, by keeping people in a state of awe, confusion, or apathy, to prevent that figure from fading into unimportance, and the priest can do this most effectively because he is confused and fanatical himself. The priest, the deist, the agnostic and the atheist all have this in common, that they dissociate God from human affairs in the hope that they may understand and regulate those affairs according to a scheme of their own. Such a hope is understandable – we all try to see things steady – but the tenor of the *Songs of Experience* is to show that if the scheme is inadequate and inelastic, and if it shuts out our better impulses, then it can hardly claim to be an intelligent one, and though it may allow us to see life steady it cannot assist us to see it whole. The effect is to do away with the possibility of our being surprised or delighted and the mind, disillusioned by the narrowness of its vision, can only see the world as a trivial place. It may turn its attention to the 'sweet golden clime' of the Sun-flower in the hope of finding satisfaction elsewhere or it may resign itself to exclusion and boredom without promise of anything better, but there is little to choose between such negative attitudes. The resigned attitude taken up by the speaker in *The Fly* is not very different to the rejection announced in *To Tirzah*, though the one poem is rationalist and agnostic, while the other is ostensibly Christian.

THE FLY

Little Fly
Thy summers play.
My thoughtless hand
Has brush'd away.

Am not I
A fly like thee?
Or art not thou
A man like me?

For I dance
And drink & sing:
Till some blind hand
Shall brush my wing.

If thought is life
And strength & breath:
And the want
Of thought is death;

Then am I
A happy fly,
If I live.
Or if I die.

The speaker has deprived the fly of its life without premeditated thought, automatically brushing it from existence, and now that he does think about the incident he sees it as a paradigm of the workings of the universe. All things go ignorantly on, following their own bent and interests, but all are destroyed ultimately by other things, also solely intent on their own activities. Life, for the fly, is a 'summers play' – is a brief affair of no great significance, conducted without knowledge of larger issues or of the end of all life. The microbe kills the man simply in following its own nature, just as the man exterminates the fly, or the wind mechanically erodes a stone away. Each nature is different, but they have this in common, that each knows only the way in which it is set to work, and pursues that way in ignorance of any overall plan – if there is any such plan. The 'blind hand' that will eventually 'brush' the 'wing' of the speaker is not necessarily the hand of a God and, if it is, then it is a God who acts blindly through the mechanism of his creation without regard to individual cases. Anyway, the speaker can know nothing about such matters, only speculate idly about them. He is like the fly, a giddy creature which 'dances' and 'sings' in its own limited way. The human way is the way of 'thought', so we 'dance' and 'sing' by speculating, as the speaker speculates now, but it does not allow us to see very much. The fly helplessly does what it is obliged to do as a fly, and that is all it knows about, and the man is helpless in the same way, acting by reflex – hence the dead fly.

The speaker dismisses 'thought' as trivial, as being his way of 'dancing', and he cannot find much to choose between the fly's way of life and his own:

> Am not I
> A fly like thee?
> Or art not thou
> A man like me?

Both creatures are monads – isolated entities automatically doing what they must do – and so their activities have equal significance, or are equally insignificant. But the thought in the poem does not develop this view consistently. If thought is as self-contained and helpless as the speaker claims, then he is illogical in finding, as he does, a general truth in the ideas which are its outcome. He cannot fairly claim to know about anything beyond himself and yet he makes a very confident assertion about the operation of the universe. Like the speaker in *To Tirzah*, the persona of this song is more interested in 'ultimate reality' than in the possibilities of his immediate situation as a human being, and it is probably for this reason that he sets so low an estimate on human capacities. His nature is to think, thinking is his 'life' and 'strength and breath', and he amounts to no more than that. The most obvious part of life is the conscious mind, and so the speaker discounts the intuitions and perceptions which, far from isolating us, dissolve the barrier between the deliberative mind and the realms within us and beyond us. He fails to see that the mind, uninformed by its life in a man and in a world, is a vacuum, or if he sees that the mind is informed, he fails to see the liveliness of the process and regards the world as, in effect, a vacuum. His thinking, unlike that of the Piper (p. 40), does not reveal the depths of his being and, unlike that of the Bard (p. 46), does not reveal an apprehension of providence, but is ratiocinative, self-contained and mechanical, and so he is like the fly in living and in dying. The fly buzzes about because it cannot help doing so, and it cannot help ceasing its activity in death. Likewise the man thinks in a reflex way and cannot stop doing so while alive and awake, any more than he could continue to think when he, in his turn, has been swatted. He is:

> A happy fly,
> If I live.
> Or if I die.

The speaker preaches one of the philosophies of isolation, presumably because he is, like the other speakers in the *Songs of Experience*, in a withdrawn and lonely condition. He seems cheerful enough, but only because he adopts the flippant view, while other experienced speakers are gloomy or bitter. The experienced nurse, shut off behind her 'disguise', is sickened. Behind the smug aloofness of the speaker in *To Tirzah* we detect his dislike of the flesh. Earth regards her 'wat'ry shore' as a prison where she is chained and frozen. The Sun-flower looks eternally away from her life, imprisoned from her world in contemplation of the future. The experienced mother is excluded from appreciation of her baby because her thoughts all centre on herself. The lonely wanderer in *London*, one of the *Songs of Experience*, states that:

> In every cry of every Man.
> In every Infants cry of fear.
> In every voice; in every ban.
> The mind-forg'd manacles I hear.

The sounds that come to this desolate man are indicative of the anguish of all inhabitants of the city, each shut off in himself and obliged to fabricate a pseudo-individuality from the conventions, prohibitions, laws and codes thrust upon him by society. He lives in isolation, but has no freedom to choose to do other than what is required of a social being, though that does not mean that he will ever have an opportunity to know or love the beings around him. He must accommodate himself to abstractions and institutions, but cannot reach out to the persons whose cries of distress penetrate his solitude.

In the *Songs of Innocence*, on the other hand, speakers are not isolated wanderers through an alien world, but inhabitants and participators who gain from living in communion. The shepherd is guided in his life and accepts the guidance as a blessing, not an imposition. The innocent mothers are engrossed in their babes. The innocent chimney sweep unselfishly answers to the need of his companion. In *Spring* (p. 139) and *Laughing Song*, (p. 138) two of the *Songs of Innocence*, the speakers gladly respond to the time of the year or to the mood of their company. In *A Dream* (pp. 100–1), which might be looked on as the innocent counterpart of *The Fly*, the speaker makes the assumption that all creatures are sympathetically aware of one another's needs. *The Ecchoing Green*, which is the counterpart to *London*, depicts persons who take satisfaction in the present moment, who enter the seasons of the year or of their life with acceptance and find fulfilment. The youthful speaker participates whole-heartedly in the spring day and his holiday opportunity, but he is aware of the 'old folk' who enjoy watching the sports they can no longer play, and aware also of the 'little ones' who become weary and then go to the 'laps of their mothers' for the comfort they know they will find. The persons described are self-forgetful, sensitive and relaxed as members of a community, not of an organization as in *London*, but though they are members they are not mere ciphers, for their sense of belonging allows them freedom to express their energies, to develop individuality and independence, and to make the most of their life as it comes to them.

6

THE DISGUISES OF EXPERIENCE

In the *Songs of Innocence* the speakers have no desire to give a comprehensive account of the universe, but they know that it is a place where they belong, where their life has significance in terms of a larger whole and where benevolence and sympathetic understanding, though they may fail, represent the proper order of things. These virtues are to be exercised for their own sake so that one may participate in a meaningful world, and be fulfilled. Experienced speakers, as in *The Fly*, assert that the universe is incomprehensible, yet having made this verbal gesture, go on to make most dogmatic assumptions about the qualities of God, man and nature. God's influence is not directly felt in this world. Nature operates mechanically, for all things have fixed and predictable habits; this allows a balance to be struck between competing entities and forces, and man is no exception in the scheme. Man is a being who, under the pressure of fear and selfishness, learns to accommodate himself to his fellows and adopt the virtues that society and government impose. The experienced position is an irrational one, of course, for it discounts the fact that, on the given premises, it can know nothing of God at all; discounts the fact that the predictable factors of nature are, of necessity, abstract and interpretative, not constitutive elements; discounts the evidence of disinterested benevolence and spontaneity in human acts. Innocents (like the Shepherd) understand that they take a meaningful part in a larger movement, and that their active participation gives them life, freedom and individuality, while experienced speakers (in *Infant Sorrow*, for example) assume, not very reasonably, that, though they act in a reflex and determined way, they are in command of their separated existence – that if not purposeful, they are wilful, and are forced to make their own way against an antagonistic world. To be individual is to succeed in accommodating the world to one's will, and to be free is to be like God, subject to no influence whatever. So individuality and freedom are virtually impossible. Experience holds itself to be completely in command of itself and, at the same time, gives that self no room to manoeuvre because social and biological necessities so strictly limit the choices that can be made that life is a passive affair. Thus the speaker in *The Fly* is very much in control of himself – he *is* his conscious mind – and makes a clear formulation of his situation, but states, also, that his isolated self, like the fly, must passively accept what fate has in store. There is a contradiction here because it is impossible to see, if the fate of the man is determined, why his thought should not be determined too – impossible to see how he can claim the independence of mind he supposes he has. The contradiction seen here is illustrated more clearly in *The Clod & the Pebble*, one of the *Songs of Experience*.

The CLOD & the PEBBLE

> Love seeketh not Itself to please.
> Nor for itself hath any care:
> But for another gives its ease.
> And builds a Heaven in Hells despair.
>
> So sang a little Clod of Clay
> Trodden with the cattles feet:
> But a Pebble of the brook.
> Warbled out these metres meet.
>
> Love seeketh only Self to please.
> To bind another to Its delight:
> Joys in anothers loss of ease.
> And builds a Hell in Heavens despite.

Blake's illustration to this poem shows the life of the brook. At the head of the poem cattle and sheep are seen drinking its waters, and below the text are frogs, water-plants, a duck and a worm. All these creatures are alive, though they do not think about being so, in contrast to the clod and pebble who are inanimate but give their view of life's purpose. They talk of love, but their notion of love is indicative, for each of them, of the limits they set up for all their activities. The clod is determined to be accommodating at all costs, has no thoughts for itself but 'for another gives its ease', and takes all things in humility and effacement. The pebble, by contrast, thinks only of itself, loves for the sake of the gratification it can receive, and is more likely to bruise the feet of the cattle than act as a passive carpet for them. Perhaps the clod is more worthy than the pebble in its manner of loving, as the latter is possessive, jealous, enjoys the exercise of power, and is capable, even, of cruelty, while the clod is utterly unselfish; but neither clod nor pebble is really admirable. Too great a degree of submission is as much a fault as an arrogant selfishness, for not only does it encourage the pebbles of the world to become tyrants (which is not good for them), but it prevents the clod from being critically alive and prevents it from ever taking a spirited stand (which is not good for the clod). Even the most patient lover should be prepared to rebel when his patience is taken advantage of, or he does a disservice to both himself and his beloved.

Clod and pebble state opposed notions of love, and Blake presents them as opposed 'personalities'. The clod is plastic, takes the imprint of one hoof and retains it until the next hoof comes. It merely submits to others and cannot be said to have any wishes of its own. It has no 'care' for itself, and is so inclined to 'give its ease' for 'another' that its love must be quite undiscriminating. As long as it is being squashed underfoot it is satisfied, and is too supine to mind what foot does the squashing. The pebble is as rigid and formed as the clod is yielding and shapeless. Other things must give way to it, for it will accommodate itself to nothing and though it can hurt, it cannot itself be hurt. As a 'lover' it has no thought but for its own 'ease'.

The clod has too little individuality to be said to love at all. It may be initially comfortable to live with, being plastic and yielding, but its clammy and clinging quality must eventually lead to disgust. No fire could be struck from this creature which resists nothing and retains nothing for long. It is all receptivity, and if it has too little character to love it has also too little character to think, for that activity requires a firm structure of mind. There is no continuity to the clod, which stupidly takes one impression after another without establishing any connexion between them. Its confused state of mind makes it impossible, also, that it should perceive anything, even though it is the epitome of receptivity. Apparently all influences can come to it easily, but they cannot mean anything to a mindless creature. No perception can be said to take place unless the influences of the world have effect on a being capable of actively giving them their proper shape.

In spite of their protestations, the clod has too little integrity to be able to love, and the pebble has too little sympathy, the one being formless and the other being highly organized, rigid, self-contained. Love is an exchange between individuals, and while the clod lacks individuality and can give nothing, the pebble is so obstinately individual that it can receive nothing – it cannot love in any significant way, it takes no impressions and it cannot perceive. It contains a system, a little world of its own; it exists in a larger world but has no intercourse in it and takes no effect from it. It is quite master of itself and of its thoughts, and because its thoughts can be modified by nothing beyond itself but are bound in their crystalline lattice it can think to no purpose. Significant thought does not involve the elaboration of isolated systems, lifeless because starved of nourishment from without, just as significant perception does not take place without the mind bringing the world alive. Although we think of our senses as designed merely to record, they can do so only because we are intelligent (in the organizing sense of the word), and though we picture our mind as designed merely to think, it does so only because we are intelligent (in the receptive sense of the word).

Blake's poem does not depict two different personalities leading different sorts of life, but exhibits contradictory beliefs simultaneously entertained in Experience, when men suppose that they are servile in respect of their senses, which simply convey a copy of that which is without, and tyrannical in respect of their mind, which is in sole control of the realm within. This can only be true of a being who is acquainted with nothing but stereotypes – stereotypes of perception and stereotypes of thought – so that knowing and creating never take place, and life is led in a realm where fancies come and go and reorder themselves, but are eternally the same. In better realms, thinking and perceiving are organically related in an imaginative and creative activity so that the mind grows and the world develops. Clod and pebble are dead things, put to shame by the lowliest forms of life; living in Heaven or Hell but quite out of touch with the universe in which they are placed. Elsewhere, Blake uses an image, related to that of clod and pebble, which gives a different picture of the possibilities of life. Oothoon, the heroine of *Visions of the Daughters of Albion*, one of Blake's longer poems, evokes a severe smile from her jealous husband, whereupon

> her soul reflects the smile
> As the clear spring, muddied with feet of beasts,
> grows pure and smiles.
>
> (ll. 41 and 2)

The spring is unlike the clod in having an identity of its own and, though it is affected by the 'cattles feet', it finds its level again, the mud settles, and it returns to its own natural self. Unlike the pebble, it can be influenced; it need not be rigidly and everlastingly identical in order to be recognized as having a character. A stream has more distinctive originality than a stone because it can be stirred and because it takes so much from beyond itself: light, shadows, reflections, glimpses of objects through the water, ripples of wind on the surface, all make it fascinating, but all are part of its constitution. The clod and the pebble are not fascinating objects – the one has no identity and the other is without complexity, so that they cannot participate in the manner of the stream or (for example) of the innocent mother in *A Cradle Song*, but are lumpish objects set apart from the flow of life. They represent the hopelessness and the arrogance which are characteristics of the isolated experienced mind.

In examining the *Songs of Experience* we have often seen the notion of the rigidity and efficacy of the will entertained at the same time as a notion of the helplessness and dependence of the personality. Such ideas are implicit in *The Fly*; and the wanderer in the streets in *London* sees himself as forced into a rôle, but forced

to create it himself in order to establish his position in the face of
a hostile world. A similar contradiction is found in *The Voice of
the Ancient Bard*, where the mind of man is seen as being capable
of a god-like wisdom, but upon examination this wisdom is found
to be acquired in a weak and supine way. The poem is deceptive,
the Bard's words are seductive, and Blake bound the poem in with
the *Songs of Innocence* until 1815, when he transferred it to the
Songs of Experience. Perhaps even he was taken in at first by the
plausible argument in his own creation.

The Voice of the Ancient Bard.

Youth of delight come hither.
And see the opening morn.
Image of truth new born.
Doubt is fled & clouds of reason.
Dark disputes & artful teazing.
Folly is an endless maze.
Tangled roots perplex her ways.
How many have fallen there!
They stumble all night over bones of the dead
And feel they know not what but care:
And wish to lead others when they should be led

Both Blake and D. H. Lawrence are often described as being
contemptuous of the rational mind, and as seeing in it the cause of
frustration and misdirection in a world of mistaken values. If only
our better, more fundamental, impulses could have a chance, un-
distorted by the artificiality and repressiveness of our socialized
mental part, they seem to say, then how spontaneously full and
rich our lives could be. It is true that both writers are critical of
the misuse of reason and the elevation of the faculty so that it
thrusts our other faculties aside. Blake's Sun-flower (p. 16) lives
permanently in an abstract sphere of future possibilities, divorced
from present enjoyments. In *Holy Thursday* (p. 18), the experienced
speaker's moral preoccupation removes him from the events taking
place in St Paul's. The priest in *A Little Boy Lost* (p. 106) is an
inhuman monster of abstruse dogmatic conviction. *The Human*

Abstract (p. 82) traces the distortions associated with a rationalist moral philosophy. All these, however, are examples of rationality gone wrong, the fault being consequent, not on the adoption of reason, but on the failure of reason. Many of Blake's innocents are young or unlettered persons who do not attempt a conscious and explicit account of themselves, who act spontaneously without reasoning things out step by step, but whose actions, nevertheless, may be described as reasonable. The adult, especially the intellectually inclined adult, encounters greater difficulty in achieving Innocence, and attains the state less frequently, because he has a greater bulk of experience and a greater complexity of mind to bring to a state of harmony in a larger and more perplexing world. One would expect an adult, in the state of perfection called Innocence, to exhibit the faculties, not of a child, but of an intellectually collected being, and in such poems as *The Divine Image* (p. 75) and *On Anothers Sorrow* (p. 71) we encounter statements that are innocent, explicit, superbly rational in the strictest sense of the word, and cast in an abstract form. Blake's quarrel, like Lawrence's, is not with intellect but with an excessively cerebral approach to life, which stupidly supposes (as the pebble supposes) that the ratiocinative faculty can operate on its own, unrelated to the human functions which give it life: the perceptive and imaginative, the sexual, the religious. In a fully human being the mind is an organic part of the whole person, and it is a failure of the mind to suppose that it is self-sufficient.

The ancient bard has a new message of hope for 'Youth of delight' – a call to abandon the sterile ratiocination of the past with its 'Dark disputes and artful teazing'. Men have obscured the purpose of living with their 'clouds of reason' so that, instead of being able to delight in the free exercise of their energies, they confine themselves in a 'maze' of thoughts about what they should do, about what they are, about the meaning of their life. Instead of 'delight' they know only 'care' as they vex their minds amidst a perplexed tangle of half-hidden theoretical alternatives or study the findings of those, now dead, who were equally confused and groping. They 'stumble' over philosophical obstacles in the dark when they should be confident and spontaneous in the 'opening morn' of life, yet they suppose they are 'leaders', finding the way for mankind.

Blake wrote *The Voice of the Ancient Bard* at a time when many men were stirred by the promise of the French Revolution, an event which seemed, at the time, to sweep away centuries of accumulated rubbish in the form of compulsive intellectual habits, outmoded conventions, political and constitutional stereotypes and fossilized social distinctions. Mankind had an opportunity, it seemed, to start afresh and establish truth, justice and right in the place of a slavish adherence to tradition and regulation. The idea is an attractive one, and Blake wrote his poem for the *Songs of Innocence*, for it seems as if the ancient bard incites to a revolution that will recover for man his lost innocence, once reliance on 'reason' and antiquity have been shed. At a later time, however, Blake reconsidered what he had written.

Innocence is a state of grace exhibited by individuals, not a condition that can be legislated for or induced by social reform, even though certain sorts of society are more conducive to it than others. Any deliberate attempt to foster Innocence, even an attempt by an individual to induce it in himself, is destructive of the state, which is, by nature, unpremeditated and self-forgetful. Experience cannot voluntarily set aside its deliberate way of acting, and only makes itself ridiculous when it supposes it can do so, being better employed in taking its own reasoned methods seriously and perfecting them to the best of its ability, allowing moments of innocent insight to come when they can. Such moments are likely to come to the individual conscientiously exercising the powers at his command and not at all likely to come to one engaged in wishing his powers were other than they are. Innocence may be capable of spontaneously doing the right thing in the clear light of 'opening morn' without 'clouds of reason', but the ancient bard's call to abandon reason is a ridiculous one because his message is itself a product of 'reason' and he preaches against the very capacity which has allowed him to achieve his present insight. It is possible to grant him that the rational mind often goes wrong, can become dogmatic and short sighted, and that the solutions to man's problems found by reason are usually inappropriate by the time they come to be applied so that a new adjustment is necessary and the process is a stumbling one. But this is a necessary condition of existence, and if we are in error, as undoubtedly we are for most of the time, then the remedy does not lie in abandoning thought but in improving it.

The ancient bard calls us to set aside the tools we have and go to work with our bare hands. The 'Image of truth new born' is to accompany the 'opening morn' of a new age. This much is announced in the first two lines of the poem and the remaining lines are given over to a denunciation, in very general terms, of the past time of 'doubt', 'dispute' and 'folly'. We are not told what the new 'Image of truth' may be, and suspect that if it were disclosed it would resemble some of our old truths. Perhaps there is no new truth – the bard asks us to replace thought, but the only positive element in his message is an appeal to vague idealism, coupled with feelings of elation and optimism for the future. Like the popular evangelist he sweeps his hearers along for a while with promises of renewal, until it is discovered that his words are moving but the promise empty, and the convert must turn again to settle the problems of daily life with his old imperfect means. There are always ancient bards willing to brush aside centuries of apparently wasted effort in favour of some new faith, and they are chary of stating the exact nature of their new 'truth' because, when stated, the new way invariably suffers from the same defects as the old. The same problems must be faced and, indeed, the same solutions are given, though they are expressed in a different form. It would be a pity, then, even if we could voluntarily make the sacrifice, to throw away our knowledge of past errors and past solutions, which, if applied, might assist us to do better. What the ancient bard terms 'bones of the dead' is the tradition we rely on for whatever wisdom we do have, and to which we must add something if we are to achieve anything at all. To cut ourselves loose from that tradition is impossible and, if possible, the process would leave us helpless and stupid, devoid of our wisdom and our humanity. New systems of truth are always built on old ones simply because there is no other foundation on which to build them, and we incorporate in our new structures material from the old because our capacity to manufacture is limited. If the ancient bard had a new truth to announce we would, undoubtedly, recognize many ancient elements in it, but the structure he puts forward is built of air. Solid wisdom must be laboured for and constantly kept in repair, but the bard summons us to a wisdom that can be had simply for believing it is there. His newly recovered innocence is an artificial one, and his 'new born' truth is vague and foolish.

Blake eventually transferred *The Voice of the Ancient Bard* to the *Songs of Experience*, and two other poems have a similar history. *The Little Girl Lost* and *The Little Girl Found*, which we may regard as one poem, and *The School Boy* both started life among the *Songs of Innocence*, which were issued in 1789. When Blake added the *Songs of Experience* to his volume, probably in 1793, he moved the 'Little Girl' poems, placing them in *Songs of Experience*. It is not easy to place a definite interpretation on the poems, but the first probably describes the emergence of Lyca from childhood to maturity, the break from dependence on her parents and the discovery of the adult passions, especially those connected with sexual experience. The passions are symbolized as wild beasts of prey, lions, leopards and tigers, but the text and the illustrations to the text invite us to see the beasts as benign, like those depicted in paintings of the age of gold – keeping company with women, children, lambs and hares. Lyca's passions are innocent, but she is deeply disturbed by the knowledge that her parents are anxious about this new phase of her life. In the second poem the anxieties of Lyca's parents are described. They follow a 'fancied image' of the disasters which might befall her, and when they encounter her passionate 'beasts' are terrified until they recognize that they are gentle and not necessarily harmful. The passions may be noble and bring strength and beauty to life, and the parents come to realize this when they are reunited with their daughter, though she remains separate from them now, being depicted as asleep. It cannot be said that the parents recover a lost innocence, but they do come to a new understanding of their daughter and come to terms with her altered position in relation to themselves.

The 'Little Girl' poems were transferred to *Songs of Experience* as soon as the series was issued, but *The School Boy* was moved much later, after 1815, perhaps because Blake came to see that the apparent innocence of the speaker is flawed. The poem is a complaint against the stultifying effects of education:

> But to go to school in a summer morn
> O! it drives all joy away;
> Under a cruel eye outworn.
> The little ones spend the day.
> In sighing and dismay.

There is no doubt that education has its negative aspects, there is some truth in the boy's statement that the 'tender plants' of childhood 'are strip'd / Of their joy in the springing day', and it is understandable that the child should be insensible of the positive aspects of the schooling that keeps him away from his enjoyment of the summer. The boy pleads for a continuation of Innocence, but this is enough to cause one to doubt that he has it. True innocence does not identify itself in this way, and this 'innocent' is aware of the figure he cuts when he pathetically refers to himself as a 'little one'. He is rather knowing in his reference to the 'eye outworn', and later he shows an awareness of his position which might be proper to an experienced observer, but contains too much self-pity to belong to Innocence:

> How can the bird that is born for joy.
> Sit in a cage and sing.
> How can a child when fears annoy.
> But droop his tender wing.
> And forget his youthful spring.

The poem contains some truth, but it is not the whole truth, and even the truth it does contain is enunciated, not by an innocent speaker, but by an experienced and rather sentimental sympathizer with Innocence. Blake realized this, presumably, and moved the poem to the proper series.

The Voice of the Ancient Bard and *The School Boy* seem innocent songs until they are examined more closely. Some of the *Songs of Experience* are also plausible, and are often taken as containing statements made by Blake himself, but on closer examination it is seen that, though he might agree in a general way with the propositions contained in the poems, he is levelling the same criticism at the speakers that he more obviously does elsewhere in the series. *The Chimney Sweeper* of Experience (p. 25) and *London* (p. 116) are two poems of this sort. Blake might agree with some of the statements made in the poems, but he does not regard the speakers as being capable of unprejudiced assessment or honest self-examination, and Blake is not much interested in abstract statements, however much apparent truth they may contain.

The poet is concerned with ideas, but only with ideas as they find expression in the mouths of persons, and he examines them as manifestations of life, not as propositions for demonstration. Blake does not utter his own convictions in any of the songs (though we may infer what he thinks when we read them all together) and he very seldom speaks in his own voice. It is clear that he approves of Innocence, though he does not put forward the innocent pattern of behaviour as one that can be voluntarily adopted, and it is equally clear that he disapproves of the confined sympathies and lack of vision of Experience, though he does not suggest that we can escape from the state deliberately, only improve ourselves within its limitations. In *The Garden of Love* and *The Little Vagabond* the speakers attack the Church. It is possible that, in an abstract way, Blake might agree with what they say, and the possibility is given likelihood if we read Blake's own thoughts in his manuscript *Notebook*. But Blake printed these two poems; they are not rough jottings, he printed them as experienced songs, and so we are invited to look beneath the surface, bearing in mind the fact that experienced speakers are not always honest with themselves. We do not have to look far before doubts about the integrity of the speakers arise. In *The Garden of Love* there is a strong indictment of the Church in its approach to sexual matters, and it is difficult not to agree with the attack made, though it would be mistaken to suppose that we have, here, a brilliant analysis made by Blake, thinking well in advance of his time. The sentiments uttered were commonplaces to a man who moved in the society of William Godwin, Thomas Paine and Mary Wollstonecraft. The speaker in the poem finds that a field of activity which should be spontaneously enjoyed has been made ugly by the interference of religious notions which insist on man's guilt and shame.

The GARDEN of LOVE

I went to the Garden of Love.
And saw what I never had seen:
A Chapel was built in the midst.
Where I used to play on the green.

And the gates of this Chapel were shut,
And Thou shalt not, writ over the door;
So I turn'd to the Garden of Love,
That so many sweet flowers bore.

And I saw it was filled with graves,
And tomb-stones where flowers should be:
And Priests in black gowns were walking their rounds.
And binding with briars my joys & desires.

The speaker has known an unaffected delight in love; he has played 'on the green', but now finds 'graves' and 'tomb-stones where flowers should be'. The Church has spoiled the beauty and natural vigour of the pleasures which were once there to be enjoyed, and substituted reminders of man's mortality and eventual corruption, which are consequences of sin. In all religions there is a tendency to elevate the spiritual at the expense of the physical, and in all religions there are sects which take this tendency to an extreme, viewing the promptings of the body as low, especially the sexual urge. The effect of such notions is to breed unhealthy repugnancies, and the stress of the poem falls on this development as well as on the prohibitions imposed by the 'Chapel'. The 'Thou shalt nots' do more than restrict activity: they alter the minds of men, taking away their innocence, and substituting thorny entanglements of doubt and perplexity. The damage done by the briars is self-imposed once they have been placed.

The speaker does not emphasize the fact that the restrictions placed upon him are there by his own consent – there is no acknowledgement, here, that the manacles are 'mind-forg'd', and though one might agree that there are, in a general way, grounds for his attack on the 'Chapel', he seems to have accepted his fate in a supine manner and now turns to recrimination in order to hide his own weakness. Second-rate religious notions do breed unhealthy repugnancies, it is true, but it is also true that we are individually responsible for what we think and feel. The speaker is relating a personal history – he talks of 'my joys & desires' as being bound – and he has now reached a position where he can see what has been done to him as an evil. The tone of the poem is indignant and the 'Priests in black gowns' are sinister figures. The obvious solution is to remove the evil by changing his notions about sexual matters and so liberating himself from the prohibitions imposed by the Chapel. Presumably, he would claim that this is an impossibility: he has been infected mentally and was infected while innocent and vulnerable; he can never be the same again – the 'sweet flowers' have been uprooted. This may be true (we have seen the process taking place in *A Little Girl Lost*) but one's personal history does not come to an end because of one unpleasant insight, the fall is a process that may continue throughout life, and the speaker in this poem is resigned to its continuation. The 'Garden of Love' – sexual experience – is what one can make of it oneself, and it is most likely to be made into a pleasant place free of the 'briars' of feelings of guilt, by those who come into it unselfishly. It is ugly only to persons who use it simply for self-gratification – they do have something to be ashamed of and have only themselves to blame if it continues to be a place of 'graves and tomb-stones'. It is inevitable, also, that such persons should find restrictive religious notions at work in the Garden because, although unselfish love needs no control, it is necessary to a 'love' which has become distorted. Selfish love has something to feel guilty about, knows it instinctively, and sets up its 'Thou shalt nots' because it needs a curb. The lament in the poem for the lost flowers of Innocence is a weak one; the speaker would be better engaged in trying to come to terms with his present experienced self and, if he is capable of it, doing some gardening of his own. We are not obliged to retain second-rate religious notions when first-rate ones are available. The speaker is partly responsible for the change in the Garden of Love, but is determined to place the blame elsewhere, and his tone is one of self-righteous indignation.

The tone of *The Little Vagabond* is even more unpleasantly self-righteous and accusatory, and it is difficult to find sympathy for the speaker, even though there is some truth in what he says and though one feels pity for his wretched circumstances. The Church has found pity, and the vagrant family must often have been given shelter in the poor-house of the various parishes they pass through, but the charity is cold and must be paid for by much submission to being preached at and prayed over. The protection of an 'Alehouse', where the family might sit round the fire until morning, might cost something, but would be 'pleasant' and 'warm' and the atmosphere would be human and therefore 'healthy'. The child attacks joyless religion and has observed the austerities, repressions and disapprovals of religious bigots who would do better if they allowed a place in their thinking for the promptings of the body – if they admitted the 'Devil' as spontaneous and healthy desire instead of seeing only weakness of the flesh and self-indulgent appetite. One of Blake's illustrations to the poem depicts the vagabond family crouched round a fire in the open. The other depicts a boy or young man being comforted by an old man. As there is an aureole of light round the old man's head it is possible that the illustration represents God comforting the Devil.

It is difficult not to feel sorry for the child who is so obsessed with the petty gratifications he desires:

> But if at the Church they would give us some Ale.
> And a pleasant fire our souls to regale:
> We'd sing and we'd pray all the live-long day:
> Nor ever once wish from the Church to stray.

The Church makes itself unattractive in emphasizing man's sinfulness, and work-house schools are unpleasant when rigorous in the application of 'fasting' and 'birch', but it is to be doubted that a church of drinking parsons and permanently elated congregations would be an improvement. Insistent self-indulgence is no more a sign of health than insistent self-denial. One understands that a condition of chronic deprivation like that of the boy leads to his being haunted by the pleasures he would like to have, but one understands, also, that his craving makes him rather ugly by warping and limiting his thought. Blake underlines this aspect of the poem by giving it a rather awkward rhythm – the sort of clumsy switch in word order used by children when they force scansion onto verses made up extempore. There are unnecessary internal rhymes and lame rhymes:

> Besides I can tell where I am use'd well.
> Such usage in heaven will never do well.

Clichés occur as well as the disharmonies of a juvenile scansion:

> And we'd be as happy as birds in the spring.

In case the reader should be tempted to concur too readily with the sentiments of the child, Blake makes use of trite rhythmical devices to make us pause and subject the poem to another scrutiny. We cannot fairly expect honesty and intelligence from the speaker in his circumstances, and should not be disappointed when we fail to find them.

Experience is a state that does have its virtues, though they are virtues that must be laboured for and not achieved with the sublime ease of Innocence. We struggle to do the right thing, but are likely to find that we have miscalculated, however excellent our precepts and our reasoning, and we must perpetually allow for the mistakes we continually make. A deliberate search for perfection cannot take enough into account – its methods are clumsy and its aims and ideals too rigidly predetermined. Innocent virtue flows from the heart, its ideals are affectionate and sympathetic, inarticulate, and made for the occasion, not verbal, defined and purposive. We can never do the completely right thing by means of our experienced benevolences and when we do achieve success it is often with the wrong motives. Finally, however, it is by our experienced virtues that we are obliged to live, blind and selfish though they often are; but all men have their innocent moments, and though we cannot induce a state of Innocence in ourselves we are provided, by our glimpses of what we innocently can be, with a measure of the success of our more deliberate attempts. The measure is a vague one which provides no programme we can follow, only a sort of underlying awareness of what has been achieved in our times of sympathy, fascination and delight – an inward knowledge provided by our own history, by means of which we may evaluate our acts, and which often forces us to judge ourselves despite our attempts to suppress self-knowledge.

In all the *Songs of Experience* we are presented with speakers who are, to some extent, dogmatic, dishonest, unobservant and self-centred, though sometimes, as in *The Tyger* and *The Sick Rose*, the fascination felt by the speaker almost dispels the unimaginative clouds of experienced habit and prejudice. In other songs, as in *My Pretty Rose Tree* and *The Angel*, the speaker is dimly aware, at some level, of the falsity of the position he adopts. Both these poems deal with wrong attitudes taken up by the lover and the spoiling of the love affair in consequence.

My Pretty *ROSE TREE*

A flower was offerd to me:
Such a flower as May never bore.
But I said I've a Pretty Rose-tree.
And I passed the sweet flower o'er.

Then I went to my Pretty Rose-tree:
To tend her by day and by night.
But my Rose turned away with jealousy:
And her thorns were my only delight.

The Pretty Rose-tree is a respectable and cared-for denizen of the garden, it produces flowers regularly and is a much more reliable and steady plant than the sweet flower to which the speaker is temporarily attracted for its fresh and unusual quality. The latter is a passing infatuation, though the owner of the Rose-tree is very much taken with her for a while. However, he resists the temptation to be unfaithful to the Rose, returns to her and is well snubbed for his constancy. Poor fellow! – but then he deserves it for not having the courage to consult his own feelings in the matter. He deserves it, also, for his lack of real affection for any-one at all and his mean-minded selfishness. He is attracted to the sweet flower – one can say that much for him – but the attraction has so little force that he overrules it for a prudential reason – not because his affection for the Rose-tree is too great, but because he weighs things up and decides that he had better keep to the investment he has made. He certainly sounds very mercenary:

> But I said I've a Pretty Rose-tree.
> And I passed the sweet flower o'er.

He thinks of his advantage without feeling affection for Rose or flower and without reference to any feelings they might have. He 'passes the sweet flower o'er' rather as he might pass over goods that he decides not to buy, and then goes off in a proprietary way to his Rose-tree in order to 'tend her by day and by night'. That must make the Rose feel watched and pestered and give her reason enough for showing her thorns, but she has another reason too: she must know that there is no real affection shown her – that she is so much property. She is entitled to be jealous because she is not loved. If she knows of the sweet flower, she has been obliged to digest, with the knowledge, the awareness of her husband's magnanimity – he would make that smugly clear in some way. Even if she knows nothing of the flower she would be obliged to undergo the smug righteousness that accompanies his decision to renounce the temptation.

Blake allows his speaker to be just frank enough to discover his fault to the reader withour discovering it to himself. His vanity is such that he cannot give a positive response to either of the two women. The flower of May appeals to him because she offers her love and the Rose-tree is 'tended' simply because he owns her, but he values neither for herself. Not that he wishes to receive a positive response – the thorns of the Rose-tree are as much of a 'delight' to him as the blooms, though he would not make the admission consciously to himself. He uses the word 'delight' ironically, but it gives him away: he can feel equally righteous in deciding to 'pass o'er' the flower and in being undervalued by his wife. To feel aggrieved is a pleasure of a selfish sort, and at the end of the poem everyone has some cause for annoyance.

A Poison Tree, originally entitled *Christian Forbearance*, contains a much more frank avowal of the 'delight' of hidden resentment. The speaker is not self-critical in the sense that he deplores his own initial cowardice and eventual deliberate hypocrisy, but he is explicit enough to give a complete description of the poisoning, not only of his enemy, but of his own life, soured by suspicion and the anxieties of keeping up a pretence of friendship. His wrath is deliberately fostered in secret:

> And I waterd it in fears.
> Night & morning with my tears:
> And I sunned it with smiles.
> And with soft deceitful wiles.

Eventually he is victorious in the hidden struggle because he succeeds in getting his enemy to show his spite first – his foe is lured into taking a mean revenge, and that, morally, is the end of him. The speaker is too exultant to realize how much damage he has done himself, though he is aware that the triumph is basely taken.

There is a greater degree of self-criticism and self-reproach in *The Angel*, also of the *Songs of Experience*. The maiden Queen has protected herself from love by adopting various disguises, but now regrets that she did so because the time when she might have enjoyed love has passed away. Her disguise, though used for a different purpose, is like that of the Lilly (in the poem of that name) which enjoys the delights of love while pretending to a white unknowing virginity, unlike the Rose or the Sheep which advance their defences prematurely, presumably to invite an attack. The Rose and Sheep insist that harm is intended them, the Lilly invites love by pretending to know nothing of it, and the maiden Queen keeps her young man in order, also by pretending to be ignorant of what might be intended:

> I Dreamt a Dream! What can it mean?
> And that I was a maiden Queen:
> Guarded by an Angel mild:
> Witless woe. was neer beguil'd!

Blake's illustration to the poem shows the maiden Queen and her Angel in the rôles of Cupid and Psyche. She reclines in an attitude of woe with her arm outstretched in a way that both holds him off and caresses his cheek. Her woe invites his sympathy but restrains his advances, and serves, also, to hide from him the 'hearts delight' she feels in his presence. The consequence is that he leaves her, and she now changes her tactics to those of the Rose and the Sheep, pretending to a fear of him which once more attracts his attention. But it is now too late, for she has passed the time when she might have cared for anyone else, and the fears she assumes in order to play the coquette are translated into real fears:

> I dried my tears & armd my fears.
> With ten thousand shields and spears.

> Soon my Angel came again:
> I was arm'd, he came in vain:
> For the time of youth was fled
> And grey hairs were on my head.

The disguises of the maiden Queen are assumed in order to hide her 'hearts delight' from her lover – to protect her from his attentions, but also in order to protect her from participation, from giving herself, and perhaps even in order to protect her from a knowledge of herself and a realization of what she wants. The deceit is used against herself as well as against her Angel, and experienced concealments usually follow this defensive pattern.

In contrast to the evasions of *The Angel*, *Laughing Song* depicts rural innocence in its most artless form. The song owes something to earlier poetry in praise of the simple life – to pastoral plays and verse of the sixteenth century:

> When the painted birds laugh in the shade
> Where our table with cherries and nuts is spread
> Come live & be merry and join with me,
> To sing the sweet chorus of Ha. Ha. He.

The speaker is thoughtless, even rather self-satisfied in his gaiety, but he can let himself go, all nature seems to join in with him in his expensive mood, and his 'Come live & be merry and join with me' is less of an invitation than a generous inclusion of his audience in his feeling of slightly tipsy well-being.

Spring, which takes us into the world of a country child, also shows Innocence at its simplest, and the poem is, apparently, constructed in the most elementary way.

Spring

> Sound the Flute!
> Now it's mute.
> Birds delight
> Day and Night.
> Nightingale
> In the dale
> Lark in Sky
> Merrily
> Merrily Merrily to welcome in the Year
>
> Little Boy
> Full of joy.
> Little Girl
> Sweet and small.
> Cock does crow
> So do you.

Merry voice
Infant noise
Merrily Merrily to welcome in the Year

Little Lamb
Here I am.
Come and lick
My white neck.
Let me pull
Your soft Wool.
Let me kiss
Your soft face.
Merrily Merrily we welcome in the Year

The cadences of the poem are like those of a nursery rhyme, the words are simple and often monosyllabic, the lines are short and mostly regular, and many rhymes are perfect. But the simple forms are varied and they are beautifully fitted to the mood of the poem. The short lines recapture the excited movement of the young things of spring – the bursts of energy shown by a lamb or a lark – and the sharp sounds of a clear spring day – the crow of a cock or the shout of a child. The first two lines, with their staccato words, are wonderfully evocative of the rather forced but very clear and definite notes of the flute – an instrument that, in unskilled hands, yields either a full note or nothing at all. The stanzas lead us through the vigorous movement of the short, abrupt lines to the steadier energy of the longer refrain, which adds its glad note to the excitements preceding it.

All the creatures of the poem are very individual, each active in its own way, but all are stirred by the spring season, and their individuality is quickened by their participation, by their sensitivity to the general atmosphere and the doings of other creatures. The speakers are as much pleased with the activities that go on about them as with their own, and Blake's illustrations emphasize this. At the head of the poem he depicts a young woman holding an infant which stands on her lap and reaches out towards a flock of sheep. At the foot of the poem a child reclines among the sheep pulling the 'soft Wool' of a lamb. The first two stanzas are spoken by an adult, presumably the young mother of the illustration, while the third stanza belongs to the child, but we hardly notice that the speaker has changed. Poetically, they are brought together into one harmony, and Blake uses this device in order to indicate the strong bond of affection and mutual interest that exists between the mother and child. To emphasize this further, he makes a change in the refrain as it occurs in the last stanza, where '*we* welcome in the year'. All creatures act in independent delight, but the delight is infectious and their delight is in one another.

In spite of its apparent simplicity, Innocence knows its world and, without being introspective, knows itself and its needs. We usually associate this sort of unaffected enthusiasm with childhood or with rustic simplicity and sometimes, as in the myths of the Garden of Eden or of the Age of Gold, with the infancy of man. Poets and philosophers place an innocent man in their Utopias or look, like Wordsworth, to 'humble and rustic life because in that condition, the essential patterns of the heart find a better soil in which they can attain their maturity'. The tradition of innocent blessedness is a long established one, and Blake draws on it in writing such poems as *Laughing Song* and *Spring*, where the speakers are country folk or children – though he by no means equates Innocence with immaturity or ignorance, his intention being to indicate that the state is more easily found and more easily recognized in conditions of simplicity. Like his poetic predecessors, Blake sees that rustic and youthful persons display a grace and contentment not easily achieved by those burdened with their years and experience. Not all the persons who speak in the *Songs of Innocence* are young folk or country folk, and when they do fall into one of these categories they are never benevolently inclined simply because they know no better. Some of them, like the little black boy, know of the pains of the world as well as its joys, and some of them, like the speaker in *The Divine Image*, are capable of highly intricate ratiocination.

There is no formula for Innocence because it is a state of perfection, a fullness of experiencing in which the soul takes everything into account that need be for the occasion, and contributes to the occasion everything that is demanded of it. The balance struck is a delicate one; it is easily disturbed by irrelevancies, the least trace of wilfulness, dogmatic or tired thinking, egotism or inattention. The balance is also one that will vary with the particular circumstance, and the capabilities of the soul. One moment of childish innocence will be different to another, and we would not expect an adult in one of his innocent moments to be like a child. The qualities of mind and experience he could provide would be quite different, and the world and its situations are differently revealed to him. The innocent chimney sweeper knows a great deal more than the speakers in *The Lamb* or *A Dream* and his innocent wisdom is differently expressed. All three speakers think in a manner appropriate to their situation, but we do not find this when listening to the experienced sweeper or the little vagabond, who merely produce stereotypes of thought. We do not feel that the experienced nurse is responding to her children or to the quiet time of evening, but retreating to the gloomy recesses of her mind.

As the innocent speakers are alive to their world and at peace in it, unlike the wanderer through the streets in *London*, they are always responding anew, they know 'delight' which is infinitely variable, and their acts are spontaneous, without self-consciousness, yet satisfying. The speakers in *The Garden of Love* or *The Angel* are at war within themselves, and pitted against a hostile world. Innocence is incapable of improvement, but also incapable of deteriorating because anything short of the perfection it displays upsets its balance; it falls and is utterly destroyed as we have seen in *A Little Girl Lost*. It is capable of sympathy that catches up its whole being, and yet has no wish to meddle. It can appreciate things yet let them be and, when the times comes, let them go. It does not allow preconceptions to hinder it from seizing upon realities, yet it gives an attention to things that is wholehearted and intelligent, as in the innocent *Holy Thursday*. It is tolerant, sensitive, and self-forgetful, yet self-possessed. We can say all these things about Innocence, yet not have a key to admit us to the state, for it only comes to those who have no inclination to grasp at it.

Blake does not sentimentalize Innocence. He sees it as a possible state of the human soul, perhaps a rather hypothetical state. It certainly cannot be adopted by an act of will, but as we have all known it, and may continue to know it, it acts as a touchstone for our more deliberate acts of virtue – it acts as an ideal measure by which we unconsciously assess the value of our efforts. We may recognize the value of Innocence when we see it in others or detect its effects in ourselves, but we cannot take the state into our scheme of things. Most of us spend the greater part of our lives meeting our obligations in the deliberate and laboured ways of Experience, performing duties and following programmes that purposely exclude the possibility of much spontaneous goodness or imaginative wisdom. We cannot do better than labour to make these programmes as rationally complete and as flexible as possible. It is only while taking our experienced ideas and ex-perienced methods seriously, in the knowledge that they must always be imperfect, that a better spirit may be able to find us.

7

BLAKE'S LONGER WORKS

There are certain themes and metrical forms traditionally associated with lyrical poetry, the poet very often speaks in his own voice, and the poems are usually written as self-sufficient and independent entities. Blake is unconventional. In the *Songs*, he frequently adapts the forms of the nursery rhyme, the popular ballad, the hymn or the Sunday school prayer; hidden allusions in the poems are to books, current in his day, by such authors as Mary Wollstonecraft, Swedenborg, or Erasmus Darwin; he seldom speaks in his own voice; the individual poems describe possible human reactions, they are contrasted with each other, and together they compose a sort of drama of the human condition in which different characters speak, or one character may adopt more than one rôle. At the same time, Blake is critical – when we read the poems together we see that he is assessing the reactions made by his speakers, and though there seems an inevitability about these reactions, given the state of the speaker in each case, a judgement is implied. Blake's interest is not scientifically neutral.

All these features go to establish a character in the *Songs* that is distinctive. Taken individually, the poems appear simple in the extreme; taken together they provide an analysis of human impulses and a critique of the rationalist philosophy of the eighteenth century – a philosophy that dominates thinking to this day. Stated broadly, the rationalist, deriving his psychology from Hobbes, holds that human behaviour can be explained in terms of the impulses of greed and fear. Our greed and selfishness impel us to get as much for ourselves as we possibly can, but we come to realize that we can get more if we submit to some restraint of our desires. We fear a condition of life in which everyone may do as he likes and take what he wants, for we would be in a constant state of danger, and so we give up our desire to possess everything and we submit to the restraint of law and organized society in order to be secure in the possession of the portion we can obtain. We adopt the social virtues of justice, fairness, consideration for others, and so on, but we adopt them not because there is any natural disposition to this sort of behaviour. It is an outcome of selfishness and timidity allied with a shrewd calculation of how best to get what we can. In an attempt to give as simple an explanation of human behaviour as possible, the rationalist reduces human motives to the barest possible number, and by selecting our lowest motives, finds he can give a consistent and apparently comprehensive explanation. The explanation varies in detail and in the spirit and manner of its application, but remains basically the same, whether found in Pope's *Essay on Man*, a psychology text book on 'drives', or in Hitler's *Mein Kampf*. It is lent probability by the facts: much human behaviour can only be explained in terms of fear, greed and selfishness, and if we examine our own souls, we are likely to detect these elements there. We are likely to detect other elements, however – so Blake suggests; the rationalist explanation is altogether too simple to account for all our doings, though it may be true for many of them. Our greatest men are those in whom we recognize the ability to behave without self-interest, and our happiest times are those in which we are spontaneously caught up in an activity or in the activity of others. Children believe what they are told, not because their belief will serve some personal end, but because they trust the adult who informs them; they frequently show affection and innocent delight. In the adult, moments of innocence are more rare, perhaps, but none the less real and valuable.

In the *Songs of Experience* the speakers subscribe to a rationalist psychology, as in *The Human Abstract*, or they imply a belief in it, as in the experienced *Cradle Song* or *The Fly*. Even when no such doctrine is implied, the attitude of the speaker may be explained in terms of one, as in *Infant Sorrow*. The rationalist psychology, then, is true, but it is not true for all men at all times, and the *Songs of Innocence* describe speakers who are unselfish, disinterestedly enthusiastic, sympathetic and loving. The mother in the innocent *Cradle Song* is engrossed in her child, and the

Piper is given up to his joy in the child he encounters. In *The Ecchoing Green* the old folk and the young folk lead lives that are given significance by their being active members of an integrated community, and by their responsiveness to the seasons of the year and the seasons of life, which they accept with grace. They do not stand isolated and opposed to a world from which they must force or entice gratifications peculiar to themselves, but take delight from participation with others in a common activity, and their pleasures are without premeditated intention of personal gain. The innocent person is an inhabitant of the world, not a stranger passing through it.

The tenor of the *Songs* is not to deny the validity of the rationalist doctrine of man; the *Songs of Experience* describe a state that is only too true for most men for most of the time, and the experienced virtues of consideration, tolerance, restraint, and so on have their value, even if they are based on self-interest. But the selfist doctrine is false when it attempts, as it always does, to explain all human endeavour in the same terms, and to trace the origin of the innocent virtues to impulses that could not give them being. The rationalist invariably asserts that the selfist theory is the only possible explanation of the human virtues, presumably because it lends itself to his rather irrational assumption that men act only on calculation. All human beings, however, have known the moments of glad grace that we call Innocence and, unless they are very unfortunate, continue to know such moments throughout their lives. Affection and delight, wonder and spontaneous generosity may animate the soul, which is not moved only by estimation of personal advantage. The 'virtues of delight' traced by Blake in the *Songs of Innocence* cannot be derived from Hobbesian postulates, and the Hobbesian virtues could probably not exist if human beings did not have, in their innermost being, a knowledge of the spontaneous virtues. There is no formula for innocent virtue, but we have been moved in the innocent way, and so have an intuition of the sort of thing we can aim at in our more deliberate programmes of conduct.

The *Songs of Innocence* and the *Songs of Experience* may be enjoyed as individual poems or as separate groups of poems, but in order to appreciate Blake's full intention, the two sets should be contrasted. Blake etched and issued all his printed works himself, with the exception of the *Poetical Sketches* of 1783. The *Songs of Innocence*, which were printed before the *Songs of Experience*, bear the date 1789, and Blake continued to issue the series as a separate volume throughout his life. The *Songs of Experience* carry the date 1794, were issued in 1793 or 1794, but were never issued separately, being bound always with the *Songs of Innocence*. Most of the *Songs of Experience* are found in manuscript in Blake's *Notebook*, but it is not known when these were written, and it is not known when the plates for this series were etched. It is usually assumed that the two series, 'Innocence' and 'Experience', were engraved and composed at different periods, and that consequently they represent different phases of Blake's thinking. There is no conclusive evidence to support this view, however, and the view put forward in this work is that, no matter when the two series were composed, they form a conceptual whole, unified by a single intellectual, dramatic and critical purpose. Blake was a fine thinker, and only such a view can do full justice to the excellence of mind displayed in the *Songs*. The fact that Blake always bound the *Songs of Experience* in with the *Songs of Innocence* indicates that he meant them to be read together.

The *Songs* are unique – their purpose is original and there is nothing like them in English literature – yet the models the poet used in composing his verse are commonplace ones. Some of these models are easily identified, but some are not, simply because Blake frequently drew on writings which were current in his own day, but are now curiosities. It is easy to see that *The Shepherd* owes something to the twenty-third Psalm: 'The Lord is my shepherd . . .', or that *The Little Black Boy* draws on the Song of Solomon: 'Look not upon me, because I am black, because the sun hath looked upon me . . .' It is less easy to see that *The Little Black Boy* refers, also, to the writings of Swedenborg, a visionary writer who describes God as a sun, love as the heat of the sun, and wisdom as its light. Readers of the *Songs* who are familiar with English devotional verse might notice that some of the *Songs of Innocence* are similar in form and theme to prayers written by Isaac Watts for the use of children. Compare, for instance, Blake's:

> And all must love the human form.
> In heathen, turk or jew.
> Where Mercy. Love & Pity dwell.
> There God is dwelling too.

with Watts's:

> Lord, I ascribe it to thy grace,
> And not to chance as others do,
> That I was born of Christian race,
> And not a heathen or a jew.
>
> (*Divine Songs for Children*, 1715)

Not many readers will be in a position to observe that the two songs *The Little Boy Lost* and *The Little Boy Found* echo a story to be found in Mary Wollstonecraft's translation of C. G. Salzmann's *Elements of Morality, for the use of children*, issued in 1790. Blake etched the illustrations for this book, and adapted the tale of little Charles, who is lost in a wood at night. The boy is terrified by a tall figure which turns out to be that of a curate who leads him to safety. Blake frequently uses flowers as sexual symbols, as in *The Blossom*, *The Sick Rose* and *My Pretty Rose Tree*. He had engraved a number of plates for Erasmus Darwin's *Botanic Garden*, issued in 1791. Darwin describes the sexual parts of flowers allegorically in terms of human beings: an anther topped by six stamens might be a queen guarded by six tall warriors, and so on. Blake, no doubt with some amusement, reversed the elements in this comparison.

It is useful to be able to detect some of Blake's allusions, such as that to St Paul in *To Tirzah*, but most of his echoes are not worth tracing, especially those which emanate from minor writings of his own day. Blake's work is highly original, and though he gleaned much material from his reading, often from works which his trade as an engraver caused him to know, he melts it all down before using it. He takes hints for a story or theme, but works the hint so much to his own purpose that a knowledge of the origin of the hint does not help to reveal the significance of the poem. His significant allusions in the *Songs* are easily recognized ones, because well known, but there is little profit to be gained from identifying obscure parts of his reading which drift into his poetry as useful scraps, and cannot, therefore, be regarded as truly allusive.

To us, much of Blake's reading might seem unusual, but this is partly because the minor works of his day have fallen out of general use. He was attracted, it is true, to books that were out of the way, even peculiar, and to writers who professed to be oracular (like Swedenborg) or to have unlocked the secrets of the universe (like the Hermetic writers), but he was well acquainted with such works as the Bible, and with Chaucer, Shakespeare, Milton, Locke, Burke, and Paine. The works of Mary Wollstonecraft, William Godwin, James MacPherson, Young, Blair, Sir Joshua Reynolds are not much read now, but were well known in the late eighteenth century. Blake was a critical reader, and though he might be temporarily attracted to some anomalous author, he reacted sooner or later, as his annotations to Swedenborg's *Wisdom of Angels concerning Divine Providence* indicates. Blake, himself, could be whimsical and dogmatic, as some of his earlier gnomic writings preserved in his *Notebook* show, but he usually avoided eccentricity and obscurity in selecting material for publication in his earlier engraved works: *Songs of Innocence and of Experience* (1794), *The Book of Thel* (1789), *The Marriage of Heaven and Hell* (1790–3), and *Visions of the Daughters of Albion* (1793). The section of the *Notebook* which contains the material for the *Songs of Experience* includes many memorable lines that were never printed, either because they did not suit Blake's purpose in assembling the *Songs* or because they were personal expostulations, written down but never developed. The lines on Klopstock are an example, or the verse entitled 'An Answer to the Parson':

'Why of the sheep do you not learn peace?'
'Because I don't want you to shear my fleece.'

Blake did not altogether avoid eccentricity in the early works just mentioned, but his manner does not present any serious obstacle to his being understood. The reader soon becomes accustomed to the style, and patient attention reveals the meaning of the poems. At the same time, however, Blake was writing works which are more unusual and, in some cases, decidedly strange. In 1788 he etched an interesting series of plates entitled *There is No Natural Religion* (in two series) and *All Religions are One*. These consist of philosophic aphorisms, setting out the tenets of empiricism and contradicting them. Thus the first series commences with the statement:

Man has no notion of moral fitness but from Education.
Naturally he is only a natural organ subject to Sense.

The second set opens by affirming:

Man's perceptions are not bounded by organs of perception; he perceives more than sense (tho' ever so acute) can discover.

The aphoristic manner of writing probably owes something to Blake's reading of oracular or assertive authors and, at the time that he etched the plates, he was reading Lavater's *Aphorisms on Man*.

The 'natural religion' series is an essay in philosophy rather than in poetry. In the following year (1789), Blake wrote the first long poem in his 'prophetic' manner, an ungainly and mysterious allegory, *Tiriel*, which tells of the wanderings of an aged king who curses and destroys his children, and, before he dies, curses his parents, Har and Heva, themselves in the care of their mother, who looks after them as though they were infants. At the beginning of the poem Tiriel's wife, Myratana, is dying, and the old man addresses his sons:

'Serpents, not sons, wreathing around the bones of Tiriel!
'Ye worms of death, feasting upon your aged parent's flesh!

'Listen! & hear your mother's groans! No more accursed Sons
'She bears; she groans not at the birth of Heuxos or Yuva.
'These are the groans of death, ye serpents! These are the
                                        groans of death!
'Nourish'd with milk, ye serpents, nourish'd with mother's
                                       tears & cares!
'Look at my eyes, blind as the orbless scull among the stones!
'Look at my bald head! Hark! listen, ye serpents, listen!
'What, Myratana! What, my wife! O Soul! O Spirit! O fire!
'What, Myratana! art thou dead? Look here, ye serpents, look!
'The serpents sprung from her own bowels have drain'd her
                                       dry as this.
'Curse on your ruthless heads, for I will bury her even here!'

Interpretations have been placed upon the *Tiriel* allegory, such as that of Northrop Frye:

> Tiriel, as an individual, is a man who has spent his entire life trying to domineer over others and establish a reign of terror founded on moral virtue. The result is the self-absorption, symbolized by blindness, which in the advanced age of people with such a character becomes difficult to distinguish from insanity. He expects and loudly demands gratitude and reverence from his children because he wants to be worshipped as a god, and when his demands are answered by contempt he responds with a steady outpouring of curses . . .
>
> As Tiriel is a tyrant, and as a king is the only man who gets a real chance to be a tyrant, Tiriel is a king, and so symbolizes a society or civilization in its decline. The achievements of his maturity are behind him, and, as his children will have nothing more to do with him, he wanders in his blindness through a desert full of mocking voices, like the King of Babylon in hell who in Isiah represents the collapse of that empire. He is trying to find some kind of rejuvenation, and makes his way back to Har, his journey being an early form of Urizen's journey in Night VI of *The Four Zoas*. Har represents the unborn theory of negative innocence established by

obeying a moral law which Tiriel started out with; Tiriel himself is the dying practice of negative experience which has found that law unworkable.

(*Fearful Symmetry*, 1947, Beacon Press edn., 1962, pp. 242–3)

No doubt this explanation of the meaning of *Tiriel* may be the correct one – it is very difficult to say with works as heavily symbolic and as idiosyncratic as this. Any explanation leaves much to be accounted for – Tiriel curses his sons ineffectually at the beginning of the poem, but is more successful later when his brother Ijim carries him back home; he leaves a hundred sons and four daughters dead, and thirty sons 'moping round in guilty fears' to await death; Hela, the youngest daughter, leads Tiriel back to Har and Heva, curses her father on the way, and is herself driven mad by his curse which causes snakes to 'rise from her bedded locks and laugh among her curls'; members of this numerous family bear outlandish names: Zazel, Lotho, Clithyma, Makuth, Matha, Orcus. The reader feels that he has come across a fragment of a strange mythology but, as the remainder is unknown, bearings are difficult to find and explanations seem forced. An acquaintance with the body of the myth, which Blake in his long prophetic works was to produce later, does not always lead to increased certainty, and many readers feel that Blake's obscurity is matched only by the arbitrariness of his interpreters. Obscurity creates difficulties, however, and if interpretations of Blake seem far-fetched it is because works so involved, lengthy, portentous and singular invite a commentary that is laboured, and invariably seems inconclusive.

Tiriel would be an unsatisfactory work even if the wisdom of all the ages could be concealed beneath its dark symbolism. It lies in a shadow-land situated somewhere between literature, philosophy and theology where the light of all three disciplines is obscured. At an earlier time, Blake tried his hand at conventional literary forms. In the *Poetical Sketches* printed in 1783 are a number of poems and ballads, reminiscent of Spenser, Milton, Pope, Collins, MacPherson; also a dramatic piece, prologues and rhapsodic writings. Some of the shorter pieces are beautiful and some show originality, while the dramatic poems are excessively bombastic, laboured and derivative. The opening lines of the 'Prologue intended for King Edward the Fourth' reads as though Blake could not make up his mind between Shakespeare and the Old Testament:

> O for a voice like thunder, and a tongue
> To drown the throat of war! – when the senses
> Are shaken, and the soul is driven to madness,
> Who can stand? When the souls of the oppressed
> Fight in the troubled air that rages, who can stand?
> When the whirlwind of fury comes from the
> Throne of God, when the frowns of his countenance
> Drive the nations together, who can stand?

The passage is declamatory, strained, and in its striving for effect, simply careless, as shown by the confused metaphor in the first two lines. The promise shown in the lyrical poems of *Poetical Sketches* is offset by the laboured, imitative attempts to achieve the dramatic and rhetorical sublime in the longer pieces. They are meant to be impressive but, for the most part, succeed only in being ineptly bombastic.

Tiriel marks a new departure for Blake, who never attempted the drama again, though he imports into his prophecies some of the vices of the dramatist: strained hyperbole, inflated emotions, unnatural situations and excessive repetition. The passage from *Tiriel* quoted earlier exhibits all these faults, and adds that of obscurity, as the old man pours out his invective against his sons, repeating his 'serpents', 'worms of death', 'serpents sprung from the bowels' of the dying woman, and so on. There is no reason given for his invective, one concludes that he is the personification of some human trait, as Frye points out, but Blake does not succeed in establishing him as symbol or as human being. Shakespeare manages to make his Lear convincing as a symbol of aged frustration and fury, and yet to reveal him as a man, containing depths and capable of development. Tiriel is a personification of emotion, not a person giving utterance to his feelings. We can feel no sympathy or repugnance for a being without a history, behaving in a manner that is merely insane in its lack of known purpose or reason, as he wanders through a landscape that is altogether symbolic and surrounded by grotesque beings as improbable as himself. It seems unlikely that we are meant to feel sympathy or repugnance, but to take the significance of the persons and situations in the abstract, divorced from any circumstance resembling normal experience. Blake does, in fact, pronounce himself contemptuous of 'normal' vision:

> Now I a fourfold vision see,
> And a fourfold vision is given to me;
> 'Tis fourfold in my extreme delight
> And threefold in soft Beulah's night
> And twofold Always. May God us keep
> From Single vision & Newton's sleep!
>
> (Letter to Thomas Butts, 22 November 1802)

We do expect the poet to display the higher types of vision, no doubt, but he usually exercises his imagination, penetration or inspiration in conjunction with pedestrian modes of observation. In *Tiriel* Blake enters, or attempts to enter, a world quite remote from that we normally have to deal with, provides no landmarks, and the reader may become lost.

Higher 'vision' in Blake is always associated with abstraction; he never wrote 'naturalistically', except in some of the early *Poetical Sketches*, and the *Songs of Innocence and of Experience*, for all their straightforwardness, are not descriptive or 'concrete' lyrics. Blake generalizes or creates symbols; his nurses, sweepers, children are not particular beings and there is no attempt to give the illusion that they are. Consequently, angels, flowers and animals can enter the abstract world they inhabit without any strain. We do not take the innocent nurse, for example, to be a particular person Blake has known or imagined, but recognize her as the representative of a certain state of mind: relaxed, appreciative, understanding. She is a type – not a type of person, as some of Dickens's caricatures represent a category of men who show similarities of personality, but the type of a frame of mind, of a poise and balance that men are capable of attaining; she symbolizes the mind at one with its world. Like all the figures in the *Songs*, she is an abstraction.

Abstract though the figures in the *Songs* may be, they do refer us to the particular experiences of our lives. We know what it is to be at peace, like the innocent nurse, and we know states of anxious suspicion like the experienced nurse. Blake's vision is of a 'higher' kind – symbolic, abstract, philosophical – but he calls, and clearly calls, on vision of a 'lower' kind – direct, concrete, existential – to buttress and support his observations in the *Songs*, and these poems are wholly successful. *Tiriel* lacks a foundation; the 'higher' vision rises up on its own with no satisfying reference to the realm of experience; it develops on a void, and for most readers it cannot sustain itself. Perhaps Blake saw this and so never printed what he had written.

Blake's taste for recondite, synoptic, highly symbolic statement is exemplified in some of his early writings such as 'Then she bore Pale desire', which was written before 1777, and the taste was probably fostered by his choice of reading, especially such books of the Bible as Isaiah and Revelation; occult works such as those of Paracelsus, Boehme, and Vaughan; visionaries such as Swedenborg; aphorists like Lavater; political idealists such as Paine and Godwin; and even Spenser and Milton may have fostered the tendency. There were forces, however, that might cause the young poet to deliberately seek out writers who were pseudo-philosophers or visionaries; who claimed, like the ancient bard, to possess an 'Image of truth new born'; or who professed a knowledge of the secrets of the universe, natural and supernatural. If Blake possessed the advantages of a fine intellect and a minimal formal education, a combination that would foster originality, he possessed, also, the accompanying disadvantage: that his attempts to educate himself might lead him to writers who are doctrinaire and eccentric. The ambitious but deficient mind is attracted to the mountebank in possession of a system or- ism to explain everything, and Blake, who lacked nothing in point of intelligence, did lack the sort of training which might have made him, as a young man, avoid the literary quack. He rejected some of them after an initial attraction – Swedenborg, Paine, Godwin were all seen through – but they marked his style permanently, and he never ceased, in his longer works, to write in a portentous and revelatory manner. T. S. Eliot says of Blake:

> But if there was nothing to distract him from sincerity there were, on the other hand, the dangers to which the naked man is exposed. His philosophy, like his visions, like his insight, like his technique, was his own. And accordingly he was inclined to attach more importance to it than an artist should; this is what makes him eccentric, and makes him inclined to formlessness . . . Blake's occasional marriages of poetry and philosophy are not . . . felicitous.
>
> (*The Sacred Wood*, 1920)

Blake lived in times and circumstances which encouraged the production of revelatory writings. The American and French revolutions held out the promise of the political regeneration of man, and prophets were needed. Paine declares in *The Rights of Man* (1791) that the members of the National Assembly of France 'are the delegates of the nation in its original character', not an organized character, and assumes that man has the ability, which he is now exercising, of sloughing off institutions and habits of thought, of establishing new ones based on principles that are innate, absolute, and independent of experience, and so starting his history afresh – an idea on which Coleridge commented: 'To state it nakedly is to confute it satisfactorily.' Blake echoes Paine in *The French Revolution*, an incomplete work that was set up in type in 1791, but never issued: 'the Nation [the National Assembly of France] sat: And the triple forg'd fetters of times were unloos'd.' *The French Revolution* is a much more moving work than *Tiriel*, though written in a heightened, apocalyptic manner. Louis XVI expresses his fears of the Third Estate:

Then the King glow'd: his Nobles fold round, like
    the sun of old time quench'd in clouds;
In their darkness the King stood; his heart flam'd,
    and utter'd a withring heat, and these words
    burst forth:

'The nerves of five thousand years' ancestry tremble,
    shaking the heavens of France;
'Throbs of anguish beat on brazen war foreheads,
    they descend and look into their graves.
'I see thro' darkness, thro' clouds rolling round me,
    the spirits of ancient Kings
'Shivering over their bleached bones; round them
    their counsellors look up from the dust,
'Crying: "Hide from the living! Our bonds and our
    prisoners shout in the open field,
' "Hide in the nether earth! Hide in the bones! Sit
    obscured in the hollow scull!" '

(ll. 68–75)

The French Revolution is written in a 'tremendous' style, but the subject of the poem lends itself to this treatment, the reader can establish his bearings, and the work has novelty and vigour. The King and his Nobles are described as a sun and as clouds (rather as Milton might describe the Father) but the metaphor, though far-fetched, has point – the beneficent impulses of Louis are frustrated by the selfishness and arrogance of the nobility – and we accept the highly elevated manner as lending importance to an important occasion. Nearly all the figures in the poem may be identified as historical personages, though they are described in cosmic terms and they are given cosmic significance especially in the section describing the seven prisoners. Blake's later 'histories' drift further from the world of identifiable events into the purely cosmological. In *America* (1793), there are identifiable figures:

In the flames stood & view'd the armies drawn
    out in the sky,

Washington, Franklin, Paine, & Warren, Allen,
    Gates, & Lee,
And heard the voice of Albion's Angel give the
    thunderous command
                                        (Pl. 14, ll. 1-3)

Much of the 'action', however, is given in terms of symbols and
personifications with a function that is primarily abstract. The
spirit of revolution is seen at work, rather than the events of the
revolution itself:

Then Albion's Angel wrathful burnt
Beside the Stone of Night, and like the Eternal
    Lion's howl
In famine & war, reply'd: 'Art thou not Orc, who
    serpent-form'd
'Stands at the gate of Enitharmon to devour
    her children?
'Blasphemous Demon, Antichrist, hater of Dignities,
'Lover of wild rebellion, and transgressor of
    God's Law,
'Why dost thou come to Angel's eyes in this
    terrific form?'
                                        (Pl. 7, ll. 1-7)

In *Europe* (1794), nearly all the personae are symbolic, 'eternal'
mythic and mysterious, and even known persons are seen in their
transcendental form:

A mighty Spirit leap'd from the land of Albion,
Nam'd Newton: he siez'd the trump & blow'd the
    enormous blast!
Yellow as leaves of Autumn, the myriads of
    Angelic hosts
Fell thro' the wintry skies seeking their graves,
Rattling their hollow bones in howling and
    lamentation.
                                        (Pl. 13, ll. 4-8)

The poem deals with forces leading up to events in the 'Vineyards of red France', but historical has been altogether replaced by visionary writing.

Events of the eighteenth century encouraged revelatory writing, not only in the political, but also in the religious sphere, where a revolution had unobtrusively taken place. Twentieth-century man lives in a world which he confidently expects to understand and control. Mediaeval man lived in a world where the natural and supernatural existed together, and he found God in miracles and mysteries, as well as in relics, symbols and rites. The scientific revolution of the seventeenth and eighteenth centuries did not necessarily deny the existence of God, but did not find it convenient or necessary to predicate a deity who could interfere with the natural world in unforeseeable ways at any time. God existed as a creator who set the universe in motion, and then retired to his heaven, leaving his creation to operate under the laws he had laid down, or else he was seen as the creation itself, not a superior being capable of arbitrary interference. In either case he ceased to be problematical or a disturbance; he might be seen as giving authority to the laws of nature, but was not to be regarded as a disturber of those laws. What the eighteenth century did not see clearly was that the relegation of God to a sphere that was remote or ineffectual must lead, eventually, to his banishment; he becomes unnecessary, and deism leads to agnosticism and atheism – they did not see it, but they sensed it, and they responded to the new spirit in various ways. Perhaps it is as a reaction against the confident assumptions of the 'age of enlightenment', and against the threat to the spiritual life, that several poets of Blake's time undertook to construct allegories of their own or to reconstruct old myths. They were, perhaps, reviving the impulse to create mysteries and symbols, active in the Middle Ages, and crushed by the Reformation and the Enlightenment. Blake, Keats, Byron and Shelley all wrote allegories in a visionary style, dealing with 'eternal' themes, and in all their attempts there is an element of pretentiousness, a sense that the poet is straining too hard, as might be expected of so artificial a mode of writing. Keats is more successful in his revised version of *Hyperion* than in his first

attempt, partly because his attention shifts from the cosmic theme
to his personal ambitions and struggles, but Byron's *Cain* and
Shelley's *Prometheus Unbound* are not very successful, being situated in realms of abstraction and unreality. Even Wordsworth was
moved to write a long and 'philosophical Poem, containing views
of Man, Nature and Society', and the *Prelude* may be viewed as
an attempt, not conventionally Christian, to see significances in
human life ignored by the Enlightenment. As the vehicle of
Wordsworth's allegory is his own experience, however, he achieves
a success unknown to his more ambitiously symbolic contem-
poraries. The poetic imagination at its best deals, not with philosophic or symbolic abstractions, but grounds its vision on the
real circumstances of life, and Blake is most successful when we
feel the pressure of reality behind his verses, even though they are
given an abstract cast – for this reason, the *Songs* are the finest of
his works. The longer poems nearly all have a factitious cast; there
are sections which are impressive and the underlying thought is
vigorous, but often they are simply dull or melodramatic, despite
the violence of the 'dark visions of torment' depicted.

Blake's mature works may be divided into three categories,
though with no strict demarcation between them. The *Songs*,
which form one category, are symbolic, are abstract in manner,
but refer us directly to the things of man (his mental development,
his potentialities, his life in society, his religious and sexual life),
and the symbols and personifications are drawn from our commonplace world. The more abstruse prophetic books, such as *The
Book of Urizen* (1794), *The Book of Los* (1795), *The Book of
Ahania* (1795), *Vala* (1797), *Milton* (1804–8), *Jerusalem* (1804–20),
also refer to the things of man in that they deal with the spirit of
conformity or rebellion; the restrictions of law, religion and the
scientific approach; the freedom of the imagination, and so on;
but they do not directly deal with these things: the forces are seen
as disembodied, hypostatized impulses and tendencies, and in
order to achieve this degree of disengagement Blake uses symbols
which, though anthropomorphic, belong to an imaginary realm
beyond space and time. We are presented, not with rose-trees and
chimney-sweepers set in a context which allows the reader to draw

readily on his own experience for the meaningful response, but with figures from an unknown mythology:

> But the Wine-press of Los is eastward of Golgonooza
> before the Seat
> Of Satan: Luvah laid the foundation & Urizen
> finish'd it in howling woe.
> How red the sons & daughters of Luvah! here they tread
> the grapes:
> Laughing & shouting, drunk with odours many fall
> o'erwearied,
> Drown'd in the wine is many a youth & maiden: those
> around
> Lay them on skins of Tygers & of the spotted Leopard
> & the Wild Ass
> Till they revive, or bury them in cool grots, making
> lamentation.
>
> (*Milton*, 27, 1-7)

There are echoes of Isaiah, Revelation and the Dionysian myth in the passage, but Blake is compounding these with other elements, known (Satan) and unknown (Golgonooza, Urizen, Luvah), to make up his own mythology, and in order to interpret it the reader must spend some years in research and contemplation, or turn to those who have painstakingly done so. Even then he may be disappointed in one or both of two ways: he may find the interpretation does not seem altogether to fit, and he may find that the result does not justify the effort; he is left, for his pains, with an unwieldy product, half metaphysics and half occultism. An attempt to read the poems 'for their own sake', without interpretation, is also disappointing. The reader is initially startled by the tremendous style, he comes across striking passages, but soon tires of the protracted writhings, shudderings, howlings and transformations of the titanic spectres depicted.

Blake's myth is a complex one and presents difficulties, not only because persons, situations and symbols need interpretation, but because persons have different identities in different situations, and both situations and persons are highly abstract, Here are typical paragraphs of exegesis:

> Los and Orc are called Urthona and Luvah respectively when spoken of in the context of the eternal as opposed to the temporal world. The whole four represent more or less the four aspects of God's imaginative energy, Urthona being his creative fertility, which reappears in the fallen world as Los; Tharmas his power to bring what he creates into complete existence, the first privilege lost to man at the Fall; Luvah his capacity for love and joy; and Urizen his wisdom and sense of form. Urizen is thus the unfallen or eternal name of what in the fallen world eventually becomes Satan, the dead matter which is the 'form' of nature in so far as it has any apart from life.
>
> (Northrop Frye, *Fearful Symmetry*, 1947, Beacon Press edn., p. 274)

> Yet it is not necessary to undergo physical death in order to enter immortal life, for the Gate of Paradise is everywhere; it opens into 'another principle'. There are passages in Boehme, which so describe a gate that cannot be found . . .
>
> But here we run into confusion, for the Gate of Los is at first called the Gate of Urthona, the 'eternal' form of Los. It seems that Blake early conceived a mythology in which gods of double aspect were to enact their cosmic drama. Antiquity abounds in such multiplicity; Bryant's *Mythology* gives many representations of *Janus Bifrons*; and Blake himself painted Triple Hecate. He seems in the end to have found this scheme impossible in practice (as his readers have done), the more so as there is a double duplication of the figure of Urthona. Both Urthona and the 'Spectre of Urthona' (who is sometimes Los but sometimes another figure) are profoundly obscure and imperfectly realized figures. Nevertheless, in tracing the origins of Urthona we may see Blake attempting to weld into a coherent whole several related trains of symbol.
>
> (Kathleen Raine, *Blake and Tradition*, 1968, vol. I, pp. 243–4)

As can be seen, commentaries on Blake present difficulties of their own. Once these have been overcome, however, the reader may feel misgivings, not necessarily based on any doubt about the correctness of interpretation, but on a fear that the interpretation may be only too accurate.

Blake's interest in higher vision, which admits him directly to the 'eternal', seems indulged at the expense of lower forms of vision and engagement with the 'temporal world' or, as he puts it in a note on his Laocoön engraving, 'Spiritual War: Israel deliver'd from Egypt, is Art deliver'd from Nature & Imitation'. Poets have attempted to indicate that the 'Gate of Paradise is everywhere', as T. S. Eliot indicates the moment in and out of time in the *Four Quartets* or as Wordsworth, in *The Prelude*, is aware of what is

> lost beyond the reach of thought
> And human knowledge, to the human eye
> Invisible, yet liveth to the heart.

(II, 403)

Eliot and Wordsworth are sensitive to an influence to be perceived with difficulty, they speak as human beings with human feelings, and their statements carry conviction. Blake, in the longer prophecies, does not carry conviction; he is overassertive, abstract, and the agonies of his titanic figures are symbolic, intellectual and cold, for all the strain of description. As poetry these works fail. Perhaps they have a high significance of a philosophic or religious sort for the truly initiate, but if so that significance has had little effect on the thought of the world at large.

Between the *Songs* and the prophecies stands an intermediate class of works, the third of the categories suggested earlier. In manner, these works resemble the prophecies, being symbolically abstruse, but in content they are relatively simple, fairly easily interpreted, and directly applicable to the sublunary world. Of these works, *The Book of Thel* most nearly resembles the *Songs*, *The Song of Los* (a brief politico-religious history) is most like the prophecies, while *The Marriage of Heaven and Hell*, and *Visions of the Daughters of Albion* are intermediate in style, though each has its own character. *The Marriage of Heaven and Hell*, the best known of Blake's minor prophecies, presents difficulties in the opening section ('The Argument') which is written entirely in the manner of the later prophetic works, but the difficulty is resolved by paying attention to the rest of the poem, which constitutes a manifesto of the 'Devil's party'.

The poem may be interpreted as stating that unproductive and passive men have established themselves as respectable, taking control of the civilization built up by creative and daring men; and passive men, because they know that the creative spirit is a threat to their security, have forced men of imagination and energy into the position of protest as outsiders. In 'The Argument' the 'just man' is described turning the 'barren heath' and 'perilous path' into a garden, and then being driven out into the wilds by the 'villain' – the hypocrite who walks in 'mild humility'. In the remainder of the poem, Blake, who takes the side of the just man, is obliged to be an advocate of the devil because passive man (the 'villain'), being in charge, has made conformity, restraint, inert reason, into virtues, giving them the sanction of his debased religion. He has cast energy, desire, creative reason and imagination into hell and disrepute; the villain has perverted things so that though the Bible, like other 'sacred codes', may originally have been a fine product of genius and imaginative insight, it has been distorted to permit the worship of a false God:

> Good is the passive that obeys Reason. Evil is the
> active springing from Energy.
> Good is Heaven. Evil is Hell.

> (Pl. 3)

Because respectable man wishes to follow a blind, self-enclosed, conforming reason he debases the body and its senses, declaring it evil, and (like the pebble) isolates reason as a function of the soul. To the extent that he takes the senses into account, he assumes that they are passive instruments mechanically recording data (like the clod). But 'Devils' know that 'man has no Body distinct from his Soul' and that the senses, which are 'the chief inlets of Soul in this age', are an integral part of an intelligent being, actively helping to create the world in which each creature lives. It follows that different creatures, especially those with different faculties, live in very different worlds:

How do you know but ev'ry Bird that cuts the airy way,
Is an immense world of delight, clos'd by your senses five?
(Pl. 6)

Passive man, however, thinks only of himself and assumes that his universe is the only one.

From the section entitled 'Proverbs of Hell' we may deduce the values subscribed to by 'Angels' and 'Devils'. Angels are habitually prudent while devils show restraint only if circumstances demand it – they 'Bring out number, weight & measure in a year of dearth'. Angels are burdened by feelings of guilt, of resentment, of their superiority or insufficiency, while devils are too much engaged in the enjoyment of things to dwell upon themselves. Devils are not afraid of making fools of themselves ('You never know what is enough unless you know what is more than enough'), or of admiring others ('The most sublime act is to set another before you'), or of giving of himself ('Exuberance is Beauty'); they show pride where angels show arrogance, humility not self-abasement, wisdom not craftiness, indignation not resentment, respect not servility, self-reliance not self-love, desire not lasciviousness. Devils are capable of the delight, exuberance and genius which results in life lived to its fullest, in thought at its most free, in creative activity which gives man his fulfilment; while angels, who are merely imitators, pervert the values of creative man, distort his thought and stereotype his works; and because the vigorous man might upset the 'heaven' of the angels, he is rendered innocuous in various ways: by being disregarded or declared a freak or a nuisance, a visionary or a malcontent:

The Giants who formed this world into its sensual existence, and now seem to live in it in chains, are in truth the causes of its life & the sources of all activity; but the chains are the cunning of weak and tame minds which have power to resist energy; according to the proverb, the weak in courage is strong in cunning.

Thus one portion of being is the Prolific, the other the Devouring: to the Devourer it seems as if the producer was in his chains; but it is not so, he only takes portions of existence and fancies that the whole.

But the Prolific would cease to be Prolific unless the Devourer, as a sea, received the excess of his delights.

(Pl. 17)

The prolific man is an artist, and his artistry consists in establishing once again, and with new life, what has been rendered sterile by thoughtless use and unimaginative acceptance.

Prolific man is given a number of shapes in the poem, all magnificent and all dangerous. Devourers (angels) are seen as horses, foxes, monkeys and caterpillers, but devils are tygers, lions, eagles, dragons and serpents. On plate 15, creative devils are described as dragon-men, vipers, eagle-like men, and lions of flaming fire, all transmitting knowledge 'from generation to generation'. They clear away rubbish, build palaces, melt metals for type, and what they produce is 'reciev'd by Men', takes 'the forms of books', and is made tame by being 'arranged in libraries'.

Towards the end of the poem an angel takes Blake to see hell – 'the hot burning dungeon' the poet is preparing for himself as his eternal lot. Appropriately enough their way lies through a stable, a church, a vault, a mill and a cave, all places where conformity grinds out its clichés in darkness. Below the cave they come to a 'void, boundless as a nether sky', an inverted universe symbolic of the confusion of perspective in the angelic world, where hell is heaven and heaven is hell. Here they hang suspended viewing the monsters of the void until, after the retreat of the angel, the proper perspective is restored and Blake is left, no longer upside down, on a pleasant bank, the black sun of the angelic hell transformed into the moon, and the Leviathan of that hell seen as a 'reptile' bred in the 'standing water' of the mind of the 'man who never alters his opinions'. The place that is evil and fearsome to the angel is pleasant to Blake, and the 'monstrous serpent' which is seen as a wonder of energy by the poet can only appear dangerous to the dogma-ridden angel. Blake assures the angel: 'All that we saw was owing to your metaphysics', and then forcibly takes the angel off to show him, in his turn, the 'eternal lot' he has prepared for himself. The angel's heaven proves to be merely a void between the stars, which is an illusion, however, as they find themselves back in the stable and church. Blake opens the Bible on the altar to discover in it a deep pit, for though the angels suppose the Holy Book is the way to heaven, they have, by distorting it to suit their restraints and fears, made it a path to damnation – 'the Jehovah of the Bible being no other than he who dwells in flaming fire' (Pl. 6). Once in the deep pit, they find, in contrast to the terrific shapes and powers of the nether void previously visited, a sad representation of the state of society encouraged by the angelic doctrines. Because men's desires are restrained they become unhealthy mockeries of the real thing; fear, lust, cruelty, hypocrisy and self-destruction take the place of respect, love and enthusiasm; the moralism of the angelic code leaves men without dignity, responsibility or an opportunity to realize their humanity. So Blake shows his angel a parody of mankind in the shape of chained monkeys who impose upon each other, the strong devouring the weak with an hypocritical show of fondness, while some eat even themselves. From this place they return with the 'skeleton of a body, which in the mill was Aristotle's *Analytics*', symbol of the fact that angelic man, who is devoid of the impulses of energy and delight, must subordinate all his activities to a show of abstract reason – he has nothing else to keep him decent, and even his religion is an affair of dogma and logic. A similar idea is expressed by Hobbes who states that one of the reasons for the failure of Rome was 'from bringing of the Philosophy, and doctrine of *Aristotle* into Religion, by the Schoolemen; from whence there arose so many contradictions, and absurdities, as brought the Clergy into a reputation both of Ignorance, and of Fraudulent intention' (*Leviathan* I, 12).

The Marriage of Heaven and Hell is written in a vigorously emphatic style: lordly, confident and scathingly assured – quite different from the subtly restrained manner of the *Songs*. Blake pushes himself forward, telling us what to think and appearing in the poem himself as one in possession of a superior wisdom. For all this, there is nothing smug about the poem; it is the 'voice of honest indignation' that speaks, so that for all the assumed superiority of the poet, who dines with the prophets and triumphs over the adversary angel, the poem is imbued with warmth – not the quiet glow of the *Songs* but a sharper heat of anger and conviction. The poem is human because Blake exposes his feelings and because he appeals to our feelings on a topic that concerns us in our daily lives. By comparison, the later works are inhuman, cerebral and cold; it is only infrequently that Blake engages himself personally and with warmth in the longer prophecies, and the topics presented there are conceived in remote terms. As an example: the 'Preface' and opening hymn to *Milton* ('And did those feet in ancient time') are written in the style of the *Marriage*, but the poem soon becomes 'visionary' in content and melodramatic in tone.

In the interpretation of *The Marriage* just given, the poem is viewed as a critique of a man as we know him. Other interpretations are possible, and Northrop Frye sees the poem as the announcement of an apocalypse which will 'lift the whole body to a fully imaginative plane':

> The transformation of the body into a spiritual substance is the Christian doctrine of bodily resurrection . . . There is no soul imprisoned within the body evaporating at death, but a living man armed with all the powers of his present body, infinitely expanded. The relation of soul to body is that of an oak to an acorn, not of a genie to a bottle. And there are no natural laws which the risen body must obey and no compulsory categories by which it must perceive. It is impossible to picture this except in terms of what we now see, and providing angels with wings is about as far as we can get.
>
> (*Fearful Symmetry*, Beacon Press edn., p. 194)

This apocalypse is an event that may come to any individual

(' "Whenever any Individual rejects Error & Embraces Truth, a Last Judgment passes upon that Individual" '), and the means for the resurrection are those at hand ('the apocalypse will begin by "an improvement of sensual enjoyment" '). But the apocalypse is not described simply as an awakening of dormant or stifled faculties, which a commonsense view of the *Marriage* might suppose the poem to suggest. Such an awakening would fall within the realm of 'natural laws', it would not be necessary to talk of a 'risen body' in describing it, and it would not be necessary to talk of it as 'impossible to picture . . . except in terms of what we now see' – for the ordinary terms are capable of providing all that could be wished for.

Blake, in his later works, links 'The Last Judgment' with 'Vision' and with 'Imaginative Vision': 'The Last Judgment is not Fable or Allegory, but vision. Fable or Allegory are a totally distinct & inferior kind of Poetry. Vision or Imagination is a Representation of what Eternally Exists, Really & Unchangeably' (*A Vision of the Last Judgment, Notebook*, p. 68). In expressing himself in this manner Blake means, or seems to mean, that the artist transcends normal experience to enter a mystical realm. So he is often interpreted, and even Northrop Frye who is very rational in his account of Blake's aims, talks, in the extract just quoted, of the impossibility of picturing the risen body 'except in terms of what we now see', speaking as if the risen body, though rising in time and in life, entered a supernatural world, better fitted for description in terms of what we cannot see. This is something different to the sort of discovery attributed to the artist by D. H. Lawrence:

> Man is always, all the time and for ever on the brink of the unknown. The minute you realize this, you prick your ears in alarm. And the minute any man steps alone, with his whole naked self, emotional and mental, into the everlasting hinterland of consciousness, you hate him and you wonder over him. Why can't he stay cozily playing word-games around the camp fire?
>
> (*Phoenix*, 1961 edn., p. 323)

As far as Lawrence is concerned, most men do not see at all, being blinded by their prejudices, inhibitions, stereotyped expectations, and lazy or dogmatic habits of mind. The artist overcomes these disabilities in order to exercise his perceptions, but this is a restoration of what has been lost and a return to normality, not an escape into a realm beyond the normal. It is imperceptive man who is abnormal, and it is suggested in the analysis we have given that in *The Marriage* Blake is describing his Devourers (his angels, with their perceptions bound by their 'reason') as abnormal; and his Producers (his devils) as being normal because they retain their unity of body and mind, and because their senses are alive. This seems the simpler interpretation of *The Marriage*, an interpretation that accords to it the simplicity of aim seen in the *Songs*, and frees it from the difficulties of the longer prophecies. Frye may have an accurate interpretation of Blake's aim in writing the longer works, but it does not seem necessary to read the same complex aim into *The Marriage of Heaven and Hell*.

8

'THE BOOK OF THEL'

The Book of Thel has been more heavily smothered in complex explanation than *The Marriage*, though it is possible to take the poem very simply. There are various interpretations of the work, but one that is frequently encountered, modified in various ways, holds that Thel is an unborn soul who has a particular view of earthly existence (that it is a degradation), is then presented with another view (that God loves things below as well as things above), and is finally offered an opportunity to view the material world before deciding whether she would like to be born or not. On this view of the poem, the subterranean land and grave visited by Thel represents life in the flesh. When she understands the restrictions she will be subject to in the body, Thel returns in horror to the spiritual realm. This interpretation presents the difficulty that Thel, at the beginning of the poem, laments as though she were already born, and longs for the spiritual realm while in the flesh; a more serious objection to the interpretation is that it limits the appeal of the poem by giving it a theosophic cast. I shall suggest a simpler view, though it would be of advantage to look first at one of the more complex interpretations, for the sake of the light this sheds on Blake's way of transmuting the raw material from which he constructed his poetry.

Kathleen Raine, in her work *Blake and Tradition* (Princeton, 1968) shows that Blake was well versed in various occult writers and particularly (as far as *The Book of Thel* is concerned) in the writing of two schools, the Neoplatonic and the alchemical:

> The theme of the poem – one to which Blake was often to return – is a debate between the Neoplatonic and the alchemical philosophies. To Plotinus and Porphyry [Neoplatonic writers] matter is evil, and the soul's descent into the body a death from eternity incurred by sin or folly. 'A dry soul is

the wisest', and refuses the descent. But the Paracelsan [alchemical] philosophy is based upon the monism of the Smaragdine Table of Hermes, 'That which is beneath is like that which is above'.

(Vol. I, p. 99)

Miss Raine traces allusions in *Thel* to these writers as well as to Spenser, Cornelius Agrippa, and Thomas Vaughan, and describes Blake's debt to Dr Johnson and James Macpherson. It is possible here to give only a very brief résumé of some of the allusions, and the reader is directed to chapter 4 of *Blake and Tradition* for the full account. Thel is seen as a soul waiting to be born, looking from her eternal world at the temporal:

Thel herself is a nymph from Porphyry's myth [the Cave of the Nymphs]; she is looking down from the Galaxy into the cave or grave of generation: Shall she descend? Can she safely entrust herself to the cycle of generation?

(Vol. I, p. 100)

Later she is permitted to do so (and to return) by the 'eternal gates' terrific porter' who lifts 'the northern bar'. The figure of the porter is traced, not to Porphyry, but to Spenser's Garden of Adonis, a place where unborn souls await generation, and which has two gates, the gates of birth and death, described by Porphyry as facing north and south, and by Spenser as being made of iron and gold (p. 100). In her opening speech Thel refers to life in watery terms: 'why fades the lotus of the water', 'Thel is like a wat'ry bow . . . like shadows in the water'; and the imagery of the poem continues in the same vein – the Lilly is a 'wat'ry weed', and so on. These references, too, are shown to be Neoplatonic in their symbolism. Spenser describes the bodily garment as 'sinful mire' because 'the soul's attraction downward toward moisture is a lapse from eternity', and Heraclitus' 'moist souls' attract to themselves the moist envelope of a physical body in descending into generation (pp. 102 and 108). Thel is associated also with Spenser's Venus, who weeps for the mutability of generated forms. Thel weeps and she is the 'daughter of beauty' – also she is the 'daughter of Mne Seraphim', a title similar to one that occurs in Cornelius Agrippa: 'Bne Seraphim (sons of the Seraphim)'. Agrippa 'defines the Seraphim as "the Intelligence of Venus", and elsewhere describes Venus as presiding over the processes of vegetation, and the Seraphim as "the fifth order of angels by which God Elohim Gibor [the cabalistic Geburah] . . . draweth forth the elements" ' (p. 103).

During the course of the poem the Neoplatonic doctrine is opposed by the alchemical arguments put forward by the Lilly, Cloud and Clod of Clay who are content to accept the transience of mortal forms and the cycle of nature, but 'Thel knows that her nature is not like theirs; for she is the soul'. She 'fears that in descending into generation she will lose her immortal nature' and 'refuses to make the descent'. She follows the advice given by Plotinus to the soul who is precipitated 'into profound and horrid darkness . . . It is here, then, that we may more truly exclaim, "Let us depart from hence, and fly to our father's delightful land" ' (p. 111).

Lilly, Cloud and Clod are alchemical, and it is shown that Thel herself may be partly drawn from alchemical allegory in Thomas Vaughan's *Lumen de Lumine*, where Philalethes is led by a feminine figure, Thalia, into a cave of earth which is 'the inmost sanctuary of nature's mysteries, where death perpetually gives place to regeneration'. The cave is 'both the grave and the womb of nature, the place where mutability recreates new life from death', and Matron Clay is the 'adamic earth' of the alchemists which 'answers to God the Father, being the foundation of every creature, as he is of the supernatural'. The alchemist regards spirit and matter as 'complementary principles, both alike rooted in the divine', unlike the Neoplatonists, for whom 'matter is mere mire, the dregs of the universe, a philosophic "non-entity" because incapable of form except as it reflects intelligibles' (p. 118). The alchemical view is put to Thel in the course of the poem:

It is right, therefore that the most eloquent statement of the harmony and marriage of heaven and earth should come from

Matron Clay, she being the anointed bride of the Most High. Vaughan is full of eloquent passages on this theme, and Blake seems to be echoing one or more of these: 'Heaven here below differs not from that above but in her Captivitie, and that above differs not from this below but in her Libertie. The one is imprisoned in the Matter, the other is freed from the grossness and impurities of it; but they are both of one and the same Nature, so that they easily unite; and hence it is that the Superior descends to the Inferior to visit, and comfort her in this sickly infectious habitation.'

(Vol. I, p. 123)

Blake and Tradition is clearly the outcome of a great deal of patient research into occult writings, including those Blake read, and there can be no doubt that Blake used the myths and symbols he discovered, just as Yeats used a symbolic notation gleaned from a similar source. It does not follow, however, from the fact that Blake was well read in the occult, that he subscribed to the principles and dogmas of occult writers. He was a painter and engraver as well as a poet; he might have found their pictorial imagery and ideas interesting without finding it necessary to take their metaphysics seriously, and I shall suggest that he used their systems for his own purposes without endorsing Neoplatonic or alchemical doctrine. We have found, in the *Songs*, that Blake subordinates his reading so entirely to his own ends that a knowledge of his 'sources' is not necessary. The same is true of *The Book of Thel*, and the poem requires attention to its tone and internal logic rather than to its origins. Miss Raine suggests that Blake engaged in a struggle of commitment between the Neoplatonic and alchemical philosophies:

. . . again and again Blake in his later writings returns to the inconsolable lament of Thel, of the soul imprisoned in a mortal body; but *The Marriage of Heaven and Hell* is a manifesto of the [alchemical] philosophy of Paracelsus and Boehme, of the 'one thing' in which contraries are resolved, and this philosophy was the one Blake seems finally to have preferred, though not without vacillation.

(Vol. I, p. 100)

Commenting on the final section of *Thel* ('Why cannot the Ear . . .' etc.), Miss Raine says:

> This is certainly the Platonic and not the alchemical view of the body. The fact of the soul's confinement in a temporal body was at all times terrible to Blake, and in this he was at least consistent in all his writings. He returns to the horror of incarceration in many passages all written in the spirit of Thel.
>
> (Vol. I, p. 120)

The final section of the poem, however, is written not without irony, and other passages 'written in the spirit of Thel' have a similar ironic intention. The passage is obscure, it may be interpreted quite differently, and one does not easily associate Blake with feelings of horror for 'the fact of the soul's confinement in a temporal body'. Occult philosophies are, for most people, a matter of curiosity or indifference except to the degree that they may influence practical affairs, and it is difficult to believe that a man of Blake's attainment should attach importance to any of them for its own sake. Miss Raine believes that he did, thus diminishing the poet's intellectual stature; she diminishes, also, his poetic stature:

> His reading of Porphyry must have brought him the realization – one may say revelation – of the true nature of the symbols used by poets already known to him . . .
>
> (Vol. I, p. 99)

The suggestion is that Blake discovered how to interpret symbols in terms of a traditional body of knowledge, but the best poets do not work in this way; their images are flexible, change significance in various contexts and discover new directions on different occasions. The Neoplatonists and alchemists ascribed a fixed significance to their symbols, and to assume that Blake was prepared to accept such limitations is to rob him of his poetic function.

It seems strained to interpret *Thel* as a metaphysical debate seriously undertaken, and there is strain in another common interpretation: that the poem describes the refusal of an innocent soul to enter the state of Experience. Such a refusal is an impossibility, and to undertake a decision in such a matter would be to announce that Innocence had been already lost. Thel is no innocent, unless one takes Innocence to mean a rather self-conscious naïveté, and we have seen that it means anything but that.

Thel is a poem of great charm – also of great humour, and the humour is derived partly from the extent to which the poem has deliberately been made charming. Thel has been described as a Dresden china shepherdess, and the creatures she converses with are presented with a sure but delicate touch to bring out their fragility, prettiness, and a degree of artificiality exactly suited to the occasion. The Lilly is, 'So weak, the gilded butterfly scarce perches on my head'. In order to point out her tenderness, the 'humble grass' pictures herself in a situation that is highly decorative. By its lightness, the butterfly helps 'the little virgin of the peaceful valley' to make her point, and by its beauty helps in the making of her dainty toilette. The Cloud describes his condensation as dew:

'Unseen descending, weight my light wings upon balmy flowers,
'And court the fair-eyed dew to take me to her shining tent:
'The weeping virgin, trembling kneels before the risen sun,
'Till we arise link'd in a golden band and never part,
'But walk united, bearing food to all our tender flowers.'

(Pl. 3, l. 12)

The cloud explains that he has a 'use' which causes him to lose his identity, but in doing so he is married to another form. His 'passing away' becomes a ritual courtship in a landscape where nature is emblematic and magical. The flowers are real – 'balmy' and 'tender' – but are also an emblazonry; the cloud is 'light winged', a faerie wooing a 'fair-eyed' virgin who lives in a 'shining tent', half reminiscent of the heraldry of knightly pavilions and half of gossamer dwellings in fairy land; the 'risen sun' is indicative of the freshness of dewy morning, but also, in its association with the 'golden band' of marriage and the early light of day, adds a jewelled brilliance to the scene. To the simplicity of these creatures of nature Blake adds the polish of artifice. Even the Clod of Clay describes herself in a ceremonial rôle:

'But he, that loves the lowly, pours his oil upon my head,
'And kisses me, and binds his nuptial bands around my breast,
'And says: "Thou mother of my children, I have loved thee
' "And I have given thee a crown that none can take away."
'But how this is, sweet maid, I know not, and I cannot know;
'I ponder, and I cannot ponder; yet I live and love.'

(Pl. 5, ll. 1–6)

All the creatures addressed by Thel display artlessness yet take up graceful postures, the Clod of Clay showing the greatest degree of plainness and the least degree of consciousness of being graceful. She confesses that she cannot explain her love or her marriage but is very sure of what she does know: that she is blessed and that her fulfilment lies in her fondness for her children. Her humility lies in complete acceptance of herself and her situation, not in any feeling of being inferior. Even though she says, 'Thou seest me the meanest thing, and so I am indeed', there is no self-deprecation in the remark, and in her sense of the honour done her in being chosen as the bride of the most high there is no self-esteem – she 'lives not for herself', even though she is anointed and crowned.

There is much in *Thel* that is formal, ceremonious, polished, 'legendary'. The cloud 'scatters its bright beauty thro' the humid air' as though a rite were being performed, and, in his association with bright gold, steeds, and a throne, brings royal pageantry into the poem. Thel is a pastoral figure, a queen dressed in white; she converses with the creatures of nature; the atmosphere of the fable is evoked by reference to unknown places and persons: the river

of Adona, the vales of Har, Luvah's horses, the northern bar. All
these features heighten our sense of artifice in the verse though
without detracting from the freshness of Lilly, Cloud and Clod –
their simplicity is emphasized by the unassuming way in which they
play a rôle which is set for them. They have been cast in a part but
the part is their life, they do not attempt to step beyond it, and
they know their lines perfectly because no other lines are possible.
Lilly and Cloud answer Thel with the same confident assurance
shown by the Clod because they say what their nature demands,
though they also say what is demanded by Blake, the artificer who
creates this formal little comedy. Thus the Cloud, who is given up
as dew to the benefit of living things says, 'Everything that lives/
Lives not alone nor for itself', but the Lilly says more than nature
has determined when she claims a life in eternity.

Some artifice accompanies the presentation of Lilly, Cloud and
Clod, but in the case of Thel artifice springs from Thel herself,
and so we are aware of it as artificiality – perhaps that is because
she is the only human being in the poem. Lilly and Cloud enjoy
being graceful, but in a selfless way; Thel strikes a pose, she finds
herself interesting and she is capable of being confused and un-
truthful – a capacity not shared by the other figures in the story.
She acts a part, but acts it from choice, plays to the gallery of herself, and Blake treats her with some amusement and a gentle
satire. She is called 'pensive queen' by the cloud, and at the
beginning of the poem we are told that she:

> in paleness sought the secret air,
> To fade away like morning beauty from her mortal day.

She seeks solitude, unlike her sisters and unlike the creatures of
the poem, who are content with their lot; her choice is deliberate,
sets her apart, and while it makes her a pale and interesting sufferer
throws her thoughts and energies almost entirely upon herself.
She talks of herself in the third person throughout, conceiving her
rôle as that of a sensitive soul – tender, forlorn, easily moved to
tears – and this rôle determines not only her thoughts of herself
but her response to other creatures. Her opening words are a

lament about herself accompanied by a wish for death, though the wish, being far removed from the grim reality she is faced with at the end of the poem, conceives the event in the mildest possible terms, and as one to be followed by a meeting with God the mild intercessor:

'Ah! gentle may I lay me down, and gentle rest my head,
'And gentle sleep the sleep of death, and gentle hear the voice
'Of him that walketh in the garden in the evening time.'

(Pl. 1, l.12)

Thel is frequently referred to as 'gentle' in the course of the poem, but nowhere else does the word occur four times in two lines. She visualizes her end with some pathos, and in all her statements this element is to be found except where it is replaced by a complacent sentimentality. She is determined to be distinctive, alone, saddened; she invites consolation, though is not easily consoled, and even when the Clod convinces her that there is a source of comfort, accepts the persuasion as a new cause for the tears which are associated with her beauty: 'The daughter of beauty wip'd her pitying tears with her white veil' (5,7). To the Cloud, she says, ' "Ah! Thel is like to thee:/ I pass away: Yet I complain, and no one hears my voice" ' (3,3), making the statement partly, to emphasize the lonesomeness she has sought. Her withdrawal is rather negative, and she persists in grief after hearing his answer, though obliged to find new grounds for her claim to be set apart.

'Dost thou, O little Cloud? I fear that I am not like thee,
'For I walk thro' the vales of Har, and smell the sweetest flowers,
'But I feed not the little flowers; I hear the warbling birds,
'But I feed not the warbling birds; they fly and seek their food:
'But Thel delights in these no more, because I fade away;
'And all shall say, "Without a use this shining woman liv'd ..." '

(Pl. 3, l.17)

Her delight in the sweetness of things has not been taken away by any unpleasant event, but by an abstract consideration (that she is of service to no-one) – a consideration that centres upon herself really. Her response to the Cloud is to turn her thoughts once again to her own lorn position, and in all her responses she ends by coming back to her own case. When she does allow her attention to be caught by some other being she is inclined to talk in terms that are too fulsome, calling attention to her own tender feelings. Thus the lamb, 'Wiping his mild and meekin mouth from all contagious taints' (2,7), becomes, inadvertently, an odious little creature, and the Worm is an occasion for an effusion:

'Art thou a Worm? Image of weakness, art thou but a Worm?
'I see thee like an infant wrapped in the Lilly's leaf.
'Ah! weep not, little voice, thou canst not speak, but thou canst
    weep.
'Is this a Worm? I see thee lay helpless & naked, weeping,
'And none to answer, none to cherish thee with mother's smiles.'
                                                    (Pl. 4, l.2)

Thel is very easily moved, and is moved too far, so that her pity, like her desolation, seems rather affected.

Lilly, Cloud and Clod appear in the poem, speak their limited parts with great virtuosity, but without affectation, then go about their normal business. Perhaps they are figures of fancy manufactured by Thel, but if so she cannot falsify them as she falsifies her own position. They are content to be themselves, unlike Thel who is without contentment and has forgotten who she is. She has made up a rôle for herself, and during the course of the poem makes various guesses about her place in the cosmos, all consistent with the rôle but all unrealistic and quite incompatible with each other. At the end of the poem, when she discovers her error, or has the knowledge of it thrust upon her by listening to what she might say after death, she is horrified and rushes back, presumably in order to embrace some of the life she has missed.

Thel's opening statement concludes with her gentle wish for gentle death when she will meet God. Like the Sun-flower she longs for the 'sweet golden clime / Where the travellers journey is done' – death is to take her to some positive condition in exchange for life which is negative, unreal, less than a shadow:

'Ah! Thel is like a wat'ry bow, and like a parting cloud;
'Like a reflection in a glass; like shadows in the water;
'Like dreams of infants, like a smile upon an infant's face;
'Like the dove's voice; like transient day; like music in the air.'

(Pl.i, l. 9)

Dreams and smiles of infants, like the rainbow, the dove's voice, daylight and music, are vanishing things, and Thel places so small a value on life because it too is a passing state, unlike the eternity she longs for. She uses images that emphasize impermanence, but one notices that they are selected to enhance the impression she wishes to make – of a delicate, sad and distant beauty. The 'dove's voice', for instance, has a gentle, mournful sound, and the bird a soulful grace. Her conviction that life is unimportant is not incompatible with a sense that she is made more interesting by her finding it so – she is not to be shaken from the conviction by the words of the Lilly:

'Yet I am visited from heaven, and he that smiles on all
'Walks in the valley and each morn over me spreads his hand,
'Saying, "Rejoice, thou humble grass, thou new-born lilly flower,
' "Thou gentle maid of silent valleys and of modest brooks;
' "For thou shall be clothed in light, and fed with morning manna,
' "Till summer's heat melts thee beside the fountains and the
   springs
' "To flourish in eternal vales." Then why should Thel complain?'

(Pl.i, l. 19)

Later, Thel succumbs to this argument as it is presented by the Clod ('But he, that loves the lowly, pours his oil upon my head'), though for the moment she escapes the difficulty of meeting it. God is within the creation, blesses it and superintends it; he is to be found on earth as well as in the 'eternal vales' where nothing dies or changes – so 'why should Thel complain?' She does continue to complain however, though she must slightly shift the ground of her complaint in order to do so, giving as her reason, not the transience of life and her desire to be with her maker, but that she lives without effect on the creation. The Lilly, she says, gives herself to others, unlike Thel who dies without having contributed anything which might show that her period on earth had significance to the earth:

> Thel answer'd: 'O thou little virgin of the peaceful valley,
> 'Giving to those that cannot crave, the voiceless, the o'er tired;
> 'Thy breath doth nourish the innocent lamb, he smells thy milky garments,
> . . . .
> 'Thy wine doth purify the golden honey; thy perfume,
> 'Which thou dost scatter on every little blade of grass that springs,
> 'Revives the milked cow, & tames the fire-breathing steed.
> 'But Thel is like a faint cloud kindled at the rising sun:
> 'I vanish from my pearly throne, and who shall find my place?'
>
> (Pl.2, l. 3)

Thel is composed with great poetic skill and delicacy, and some touches are exceedingly fine, such as the description of the Lilly as 'Giving to those that cannot crave, the voiceless, the o'ertired'. Blake uses the pathetic fallacy in the poem, partly to allow Thel to enter into a series of dialogues, partly to indicate that the points of view put forward by the non-human creatures in the poem (animate and inanimate) are explanations of the workings of the universe projected by the human mind, partly in order to indicate that Thel has a tendency to be sentimental and to see things in a way that suits her own convenience. The Lilly should follow suit – it has been given a voice and an intelligence about its situation not expected in plants and so should, in its turn, ascribe emotions and thoughts to creatures and things lower in the scale of life. It certainly should be supposed to do so by Thel, who makes this sort of ascription, but she cannot falsify the Lilly, and in describing the plant she places it in relation to 'those that cannot crave, the voiceless'. This order of creatures is without intelligence or motive, and is not to be comprehended as shadowing the human mind. There are modes of existence and realms of the universe beyond man's imagining, and though Thel does not really know this, she cannot help allowing the knowledge to the Lilly – a more truthful creature. The Lilly is content to be itself and allows others to be what they are without attempting to pry into them. Thel, on the other hand, projects her ideas on to everything, but is remarkably ignorant about herself, as we shall see.

The Lilly gives 'to those that cannot crave' – to creatures that are too little aware of themselves to be able, even, to give thanks or feel gratitude. The Lilly feels gratitude to her maker, but is too little aware of herself to feel that in giving she has been generous – she gives because it lies in her to do so. Thel has given nothing (so she says): 'I vanish from my pearly throne, and who shall find my place?' The statement sounds very commendable; she laments the fact that she makes no contribution, but does so, partly for the sake of complaining, partly to point out that no memento of her earthly existence remains. There is no generous impulse here, only a self-centred and self-pitying wail that contrasts with the selflessness of the modest Lilly and the simplicity of the 'voiceless'.

In her opening statement Thel drew no distinction between her condition and that of other beings. The 'children of the spring' like herself lived an insubstantial life that had no significance. In order to maintain her lament in the face of the Lilly's answer (that God visits the vale) she is obliged to differentiate between herself and other creatures, ascribing to them a significant rôle in the natural cycle and denying it to herself. In doing so she shifts her complaint: having directed it first against the insignificance of life she now turns it against the fact that she alone is set apart without a rôle in life. Initially, she has wished for death:

'Ah! gentle may I lay me down,'

but goes on to say to the Lilly:

> 'I vanish from my pearly throne, and who shall find my place?'

To the Cloud she continues in the same vein:

> 'I pass away: yet I complain, and no one hears my voice
> . . .',

and later changes this to:

> 'And all shall say, "Without a use this shining woman lived . . .."'

By now she has completely altered the ground of her lament, but this ground is removed when it is pointed out to her by the Cloud that she does have a use in the natural cycle:

> 'Then if thou art the food of worms, O virgin of the skies,
> 'How great thy use, how great thy blessing! Every thing that lives
> 'Lives not alone nor for itself.'
>
> (Pl. 3, l. 15)

Even though Thel is a 'virgin of the skies' (is one who is destined for immortality and one whose thoughts are on higher things), she has the same opportunities in nature as the creatures of the earth. She is part of a divine plan that takes in the whole earthly creation. The Clod pursues this line of thought:

> 'But he that loves the lowly, pours his oil upon my head,
> 'And kisses me, and binds his nuptial bands around my breast,
> 'And says "Thou mother of my children, I have loved thee . . ."'
>
> (Pl. 5, l. 1)

When this argument was presented by the Lilly in an attempt to reconcile Thel to an earthly life she evaded it by pointing out that she was different, standing apart from the cycle of nature. She can no longer do this, but she can now turn the argument to a fresh source of woe because in the course of making her answers she has completely changed the reason for her complaint, forgetting her first statement and, in fact, denying that she made it:

> 'That God would love a Worm I knew, and punish the evil
>   foot
> 'That wilful bruis'd its helpless form; but that he cherish'd
>   it
> 'With milk and oil I never knew, and therefore did I weep;
> 'And I complain'd in the mild air, because I fade away,
> 'And lay me down in thy cold bed, and leave my shining lot'.
>
> (Pl. 5, l. 9)

God does not dwell apart in the skies as a remote judge, but dwells within the creation too – she has been persuaded of that, but she has also persuaded herself that she grieved because she is destined to die. In fact, her original complaint was that she was obliged to live, and death did not come quickly enough to suit her:

> 'Ah! gentle may I lay me down, and gentle rest my head,
> 'And gentle sleep the sleep of death, and gentle hear the
>   voice
> 'Of him that walketh in the garden in the evening time.'
>
> (Pl. 1, l. 12)

But Thel has forgotten that. She has a new way of being pathetic (she must die), though in an attempt to appear consistent she is obliged to assume that she had been saddened by this all along – a lie that she believes herself.

Thel moves from a position in which she subscribes to the idea that life is meaningless, and so regrets that she must live, to the opposite position in which, subscribing to the idea that life is meaningful, she can regret that she must die. Presumably she is

now ready to complete the cycle, argue her way back to her initial
position, and so go on endlessly round in a circle. She may, for
instance, consider the fact that, as food for worms, it is only by
dying that she participates in God's natural cycle and so be
enabled to complain that her time alive is spiritually insignificant.
She could then allow herself to be persuaded that she is nevertheless an immortal soul and having established that, and forgetting
the steps by which she did so, proceed to bemoan her life on
earth, thus coming back to her first lament. There are other ways
in which she could keep it up – the point being that her metaphysical speculations (if they can be called that) are artificial,
naïve and vain. She is depicted as one who withdraws, fading
away 'like morning beauty from her mortal day', and she spends
her time in self-centred and pointless musings about her place in
the cosmos, instead of enjoying the gifts she has been endowed
with. She misuses her human intelligence by exercising it in
pseudo-philosophical speculation about the transcendental –
speculation which can lead to no final result, merely to a self-
deceiving fluctuation between incompatible and irrelevant
answers (life has significance – life is without significance). In
this manner Thel simply wastes her life away.

Thel is an allegory, a quaint parable setting out the extremes
between which, in his thinking about religious matters, man
fluctuates. God created the world, so how can life anywhere in his
creation be anything but good? But man fell, and all earth with
him, so our worldly life is deprived of goodness. God redeemed
mankind and his goodness is apparent here. God redeemed mankind and his goodness is apparent only in the eternal life to which
we are called. Not only the Christian, but all religions present
confident and contradictory statements disclosing God's attitude
to his creation, and the statements are accompanied by contradictory practices. By sacrament and ritual we dedicate our carnal
pursuits to God, but we also abjure the flesh. We lavish our
human art on church and temple or we regard all forms of
decoration as idolatrous. The lords of the Church are clothed in
silk while the ascetic goes nearly naked. Even God has more than
one form, being the stern judge and punisher who exists above

our sinful level, and being the man who takes our condition and intercedes for us. These contradictions cannot be resolved, though they can be explained and shown to be necessary⎣Blake implies an explanation and demonstrates the necessity in the *Songs of Innocence and of Experience*, especially in such songs as *The Divine Image, The Little Black Boy, Introduction* to Experience, *Earth's Answer* and *To Tirzah*.⎦The truly religious man takes these contradictions in his stride, knowing that theology is the creation of both man and God, just as the Church, though God's instrument, is given into man's hand, and knowing that if these things did not acquire our imperfections we could not use them. Perfect institutions and perfect knowledge could not offer a challenge to our moral being – could not test or exercise the soul.⎦

Thel avoids the exercise of her moral being by dwelling on transcendental matters. She is the amateur metaphysician interested in the unknown divine purpose – in the occult significance of her life and not in its intrinsic qualities. Her interest is similar to that of the Neoplatonic and alchemical writers referred to earlier, though she is shocked and brought back to earth at the end of the poem. Before that, she shuttles between two distinct and incompatible theories, as man is inclined to do in his religious thinking, and it is as a critique of this thinking that Blake offers the allegory. He draws on Neoplatonic and alchemical symbolism in order to construct the work, but it is not necessary to identify the exact source of the symbols in order to read his purpose or to follow the confusions in Thel's mind. Blake seized upon the two occult traditions with their accompanying symbols, probably because he found that they exemplified very clearly the opposed directions of pull he found at work in all religious philosophies. It seems unlikely that he seized upon them (if one takes into account the tone of *Thel*) because he found himself forced to take them seriously as opposing beliefs between which he was obliged to choose. Neoplatonic and alchemical philosophies are metaphysical stereotypes, it appears that Blake regarded them with some amusement, and it is with gentle humour that he depicts Thel's unreal and self-defeating adventures in the realm of transcendental speculation.

Thel wonders about cosmic affairs and supposes that she has definite knowledge about the divine intention, though certainty in such matters is not possible to mortal beings. She affects to know more than is possible and removes herself, in her affectation, from the sort of enjoyment she should have – an enjoyment that is bound up with her human senses, her human nature and limitations, and the conditions of her human existence. In the last section of the poem she discovers her mistake. She is permitted to go underground, to listen to the lament she is due to utter after death, to hear what she is missing, and she flies back to the land of the living, presumably because she has discovered that 'there is no work, nor device, nor knowledge, nor wisdom, in the grave' (Ecclesiastes 9. 10). While alive, Thel's thoughts have centred on the affairs of the spirit, and even when considering her body she thinks only of its 'use' in terms of a divine plan. Her dead voice, heard from the grave, thinks exclusively in terms of the body, enumerating and describing the senses, including the sexual 'sense', but says nothing of the divine or eternal. This section of the poem is written in an aphoristic, didactic style, reminiscent of *The Marriage of Heaven and Hell*, and echoes some of the statements found there:

Man has no Body distinct from his Soul; for that call'd Body is a portion of Soul discern'd by the five Senses, the chief inlets of Soul in this age.

Energy is the only life, and is from the Body; and Reason is the bound or outward circumference of Energy.

Energy is Eternal Delight.

Blake refuses to make a distinction between the spirit and the flesh, and the senses are an integral part of a unified being whose 'only life' is from the integral part called 'body'. The Thel who lies dead in the grave knows that the five senses are the 'chief inlets of Soul in this age', and that they are the avenues for all our knowledge: 'Why cannot the Ear be closed to its own destruction?' etc. If the senses could be closed, the human soul could not exist or come into existence; only human senses operating in a human being could give rise to human thoughts and perceptions, and the quality of the senses will vary with the quality of the individual who exercises them. Blake often returns to this theme at this period of his career, especially in *The Visions of theDaughters of Albion*:

'Ask the wild ass why he refuses burdens, and the meek
 camel
'Why he loves man: is it because of eye, ear, mouth, or skin,
'Or breathing nostrils? No, for these the wolf and tyger
 have.'

(Pl. 3, l. 7)

'How can the giver of gifts experience the delights of the
 merchant?
'How the industrious citizen the pains of the husbandman?
'How different far the fat fed hireling with hollow drum,
'Who buys whole corn fields into wastes, and sings upon the
 heath!
'How different their eye and ear! how different the world to
 them!'

(Pl. 5, l. 12)

'Does the whale worship at thy footsteps as the hungry dog;
'Or does he scent the mountain prey because his nostrils
 wide
'Draw in the ocean? does his eye discern the flying cloud
'As the raven's eye? or does he measure the expanse like the
 vulture?
'Does the still spider view the cliffs where eagles hide their
 young;
'Or does the fly rejoice because the harvest is brought in?
'Does not the eagle scorn the earth & despise the treasures
 beneath?
'But the mole knoweth what is there, & the worm shall tell it
 thee.'

(Pl. 5, l. 33)

It is by the senses that we live, but the senses are not merely passive, for they interpret the world according to what we are. The whale and the eagle have different bodies, different senses, and live in different spheres. The giver of gifts and the merchant have similar bodies and senses, and live in a similar sphere, but each enjoys the delights peculiar to himself and his senses create a world to suit his nature. The 'Motto' to *The Book of Thel* implies much the same thing:

> Does the Eagle know what is in the pit?
> Or wilt thou go ask the Mole?
> Can wisdom be put in a silver rod?
> Or Love in a golden bowl?

In the last two lines Blake refers, in his usual loose way, to well-known verses in Ecclesiastes which describe the death of the body:

> Or ever the silver cord be loosed, or the golden bowl be broken, or the pitcher be broken at the fountain, or the wheel broken at the cistern.
> Then shall the dust return to the earth as it was: and the spirit shall return unto God who gave it.

> (12.6)

Thel supposes that soul and body are distinct, as we have seen, and the Preacher may be taken to suggest the same duality, but while this assumption is a source of error in Thel, it leads to wisdom in Ecclesiastes:

> For that which befalleth the sons of men befalleth beasts; even one thing befalleth them: as the one dieth, so dieth the other; yea, they have all one breath; so that a man hath no preeminence above a beast: for all is vanity.
> . . . .
> Who knoweth the spirit of man that goeth upward, and the spirit of the beast that goeth downward to the earth?

> Wherefore I perceive that there is nothing better, than that
> a man should rejoice in his own works; for that is his portion:
> for who shall bring him to see what shall be after him?
>
> (3. 19–22)

At no point does Thel assume that she should 'rejoice in her
own works', accepting her 'portion' in ignorance of 'what shall
be after her'. Instead, she sways between different theories about
the 'spirit of man that goeth upward' and that part of her that
'goeth downward to the earth', and is ignorant of her real powers
and her proper enjoyments as an integrated soul and body.

The 'spirit of the beast' derives its vitality from an active
enjoyment of the capacities peculiar to itself; the eagle is not
curious about 'what is in the pit', but the mole knows it intimately. Can 'Wisdom be put in the silver rod' of the human body?
The inference to be drawn from the preceding two lines of the
'Motto' and from the concluding section of the poem is that the
only wisdom that can be firmly possessed by man is the wisdom
given him by his human faculties; by the 'five Senses, the chief
inlets of Soul in this age'; by the energies, including the reason,
which are 'the only life, and are from the Body'. Reason and soul
cannot be looked on as aloof and separate entities, granted an
existence apart from 'that which goeth downward to the earth',
but exist because conjoined to the flesh. Can 'Love be put in a
golden bowl' that is due, one day, to be broken? Everything that
comes to man comes not only through the body, it is only through
the body that he utters himself, and the only love he knows is of
the body in one way or another.

In the final section of the poem the voice from the grave broods
over the activities of the living body, asking questions of a quite
different sort to those put earlier by Thel – different because they
plot the inescapable facts of human existence without making
conjectures about the ultimate significance of those facts. The
questions do not require an answer; they are 'breathed in a voice
of sorrow', utter the 'why' of regret, and act as a reproach to the
living Thel for her affectations and her neglect. All verbal knowledge comes to the intelligent ear, including the knowledge,

denied to beasts, of ultimate death. The eye does not passively record inert data to be conveyed to a separate deciding mind, but interprets as it sees the 'poison' that may be within a smile. It 'graces' and 'gives' the form and order that are the 'fruits' of experience, and the imprints which are the 'coinage' of a living being forming the world as it is encountered. The 'glist'ning eye' covertly but tensely guarded by the 'fighting men' and 'arrows' of lids and lashes, and the 'fierce whirlpool' of the convoluted ear are active participants in a lively process that unites the individual to the world, ready to capture experience, defend against it or avidly 'create' what comes. Passive sense organs, analogous to a camera or a microphone, could not exist in a living being and, if they could exist, would vainly attempt to mediate between a world that was a meaningless chaos and a mind that was a sense-less blank. Thel, in making a division between 'herself' and her body, between 'herself' and her world of experience, has implicitly denied that she has any existence whatever, has turned away from her source of life in consequence, and the voice from the grave-plot laments the wasted opportunity.

The imagery of the lament asserts the interdependence of the knower and the known. The tongue receives 'from every wind', but what is received ('honey') comes in a form that is interpreted as it is taken. What the nostril takes can only be described in terms that are subjective – can only come in some apprehensible form, as though 'terror, trembling. & affright' were from without. The senses protect the individual and they involve him in his world; they make participation possible but do so by shaping that with which we participate, so that we are both formed by our world and yet form what it is. What is of the self and what lies beyond the self are two things, yet they are so intimately related and exert so profound an influence on each other that it is difficult to conceive them apart. The final reference made is to the sexual parts of man. They, too, have their 'curbs' and protections, are private to the individual but, like the senses, bring us the profound vitality of contact. Acts of love, like other acts of participation, involve the whole being and are simultaneously an intensification of the self and a giving up of the self.

'VISIONS OF THE DAUGHTERS
OF ALBION'

The Book of Thel is written in a style similar to that of the *Songs*:
the creatures we encounter might have come from the pages of
Songs of Innocence, Blake's quiet irony is only slightly more obvious
than in *Songs of Experience*, and the gentle amusement with which
Thel is regarded is similar to that seen in *The Lilly* or *My Pretty
Rose Tree*. It is only in the last section of *Thel* that there is a
change to the dark, cryptic, philosophical style associated with
the minor prophecies: *The Marriage of Heaven and Hell* and
Visions of the Daughters of Albion. The latter poem is by far the
most dark of the series we are dealing with; it is difficult, but it
develops the philosophy (or psychology) presented in the earlier
works, is consistent with them, and gives up its meaning to study,
though patience is needed. It is not necessary to bring any special
knowledge to the poem, though we shall occasionally, for the sake
of completeness, refer to some of the philosophers of the Enlightenment in the pages that follow.

There is no formula for Innocence – the qualities exhibited in
that state depend entirely on the person concerned and the
particular occasion, but we do recognize, in the innocent person,
a completeness and adequacy of intelligence, self-forgetfulness
allied with self-fulfilment, a wholeness that comes from participation. In the state of Experience division occurs in various
forms: persons are too self-centred to participate, their intelligence becomes starved and their organs of sense ineffectual; mind
and body become opposing elements struggling for the upper
hand; restraint and calculation take the place of imaginative and
responsible enjoyment. *The Book of Thel* is an extension of the
Songs of Experience, and provides a further study, perhaps, of the
Sun-flower who longs for 'that sweet golden clime / Where the
travellers journey is done', or of the Ancient Bard, intent on

ultimate reality. The poem differs from the *Songs* in the conclusion where Blake, in a series of rhetorical questions, seems to
take over the exposition. In *The Marriage of Heaven and Hell*
Blake takes over completely, denounces the Devourer (imitative
but uncreative man whom we can associate with Experience)
and praises Energy, wholeness of being, and an exuberant involvement in the creation – all qualities of Innocence. In *Visions of the
Daughters of Albion* the poet reverts to a dramatic style, allowing
the innocent Oothoon and the experienced Theotormon and
Bromion to speak in their own voices, though it is quite easy to
see where his sympathies lie. All these works are studies in
Innocence and Experience, but while the *Songs* are a fairly dispassionate study of the states of human existence taking in persons
of all ages and conditions (a critical psychology is presented), and
The Book of Thel is tolerant and amused in tone, the *Marriage* and
the *Visions*, which deal exclusively with mature men and women,
approach their subject censoriously. Blake is openly partisan in
the *Marriage*, and in the *Visions*, where he adopts an ethical rather
than a psychological point of view, his dislike of Theotormon and
Bromion is apparent.

The fragment of a story contained in the *Visions* is adapted from
Ossian's *Oithona*, and the names 'Oothoon' and 'Theotormon'
are taken from that work. There are echoes in the poem of the
Song of Solomon, of Ovid's *Metamorphoses*, of Milton's writings
on divorce, of Mary Wollstonecraft's *Rights of Women*, and of
J. G. Stedman's *Narrative of a Five Years Expedition Against the
Revolted Negroes of Surinam* (1796). Blake engraved some of the
plates for this last work, which gives an account of the conditions
of black slaves in American territories. It does not matter in the
least if the reader fails to identify Blake's sources, which are not
helpful. Perhaps he means us to see the connexion with the Song
of Solomon and to notice that Oothoon, like the Bride, asks for a
love that is without shame or jealousy. This is denied to Oothoon,
and the Daughters of Albion, unlike the Daughters of Jerusalem,
cannot assist her to find it. It is of no apparent significance that
the action of the poem is taken from *Oithona*, and the 'story',
which is told in the first forty-three lines, is meant to provide a

dramatic setting for the statements that follow – first Oothoon speaks, then Theotormon, Bromion and finally Oothoon again. Each character professes his or her beliefs, and from these beliefs we can infer the state of mind sustaining them.

In the first section of the poem Oothoon, 'the soft soul of America', wanders along the vales of Leutha. After plucking the bright Marygold she is rent by Bromion's thunders, and bound back-to-back with Bromion in his caves. Theotormon then sits on guard over the pair while Oothoon calls on his eagles to rend away her 'defiled bosom'. The symbols here seem rather arbitrarily chosen and so some of their significance is lost on the reader, but it seems, in outline, that Oothoon, overcoming her virgin fears, goes in search of her lover, is ravished by Bromion, and then punished as an adultress by Theotormon. It is apparent, from the terms used in telling the story, that it has a political meaning as well, but we will set this aspect aside for the moment in order to examine some peculiarities in the account of the sexual triangle. First, it is not clear that when Oothoon turns her face 'to where my whole soul seeks', that it is Theotormon whom she wants. On leaving the vale she encounters Bromion as if he is expected and not as if he waylays her. Secondly, though Bromion and Oothoon are an 'adulterate pair' and are punished by Theotormon, it is not clear that the pair are adulterous as well, and that Theotormon has the right to behave, as he does, in the manner of a jealous husband. Bromion says:

'Now thou maist marry Bromions harlot, and protect the child
'Of Bromions rage, that Oothoon shall put forth in nine moons time.' (Pl. 2, l. 1)

The adulterate act took place before the marriage. Thirdly, Oothoon seems to become married to both Bromion and Theotormon, being bound physically to the one while the other guards her and assumes proprietary rights over her. It should be added that Oothoon is slighted by both her 'husbands', by the one in disgust and by the other in disdain.

Bromion and Theotormon are presented in the poem and in Blake's accompanying illustrations as complementary beings, each too one-sided to be said to possess a personality. The simplest way of looking at them, a way that accounts for the anomalies in the 'marriage' triangle, is as the two aspects of a single divided being – of a man who has fallen into inconsistency and so been forced to divide himself into compartments. His 'higher' rational being (as Theotormon) is disgusted by his 'lower' animal being (as Bromion) and he punishes himself and his wife in consequence. Oothoon, on the other hand, has a single identity and enjoys life in all its complexity without falsifying her human nature. In view of the limitations of Theotormon and Bromion and the complementary nature of their statements and notions, it seems necessary, in interpreting the poem, to regard them as aspects of a divided personality, but there is other evidence that Blake intended us to see them in this way. Theotormon, Bromion and Oothoon are shown together in three of the illustrations to the poem. In one of these the two men have flowing hair and appear aged. In another they are youthful. In the full-page illustration at the end of the work all three figures are naked, the two men are bearded and they are in the prime of life. Theotormon and Bromion vary in appearance in the three illustrations, but they vary together, though each has his characteristic posture. In all the illustrations Theotormon is shown in a crouching position with his head gloomily sunk between his arms so that his senses are closed up. Bromion, on the other hand, is all sensation. His his head is raised and he is alert. In the final illustration his ears are prominent, his eyes start from his head, his mouth is wide open and his hair rises in terror. We do not see Theotormon's features, but in each illustration he bears an exact resemblance in physique to Bromion. In each instance Blake has drawn the same man in two postures, one altogether introverted and one extroverted, though this cannot be confirmed by a comparison of the faces of the men.

The bipartite nature of Theotormon (Bromion) finds an echo in *The Clod and the Pebble* of the *Songs of Experience* (discussed on pp. 119ff.) and the *Visions* might well have been written as an expanded version of that poem. Like the clod, Bromion is plastic; all perception of a debased sort; a cow's doormat taking the imprint of one hoof-mark faithfully until the next comes to squash it out. He cannot think because he has hardly any organization of his own and can only faithfully record the effects of something else. Blake depicts Bromion as composed all of sense organs, and when he recites his creed he pins his faith on sensation. Theotormon is the pebble – hard, crystalline, self-contained; an organization sufficient to itself, holding itself together but incapable of thought because it cannot take an impression from elsewhere. He is incapable of perception. He describes himself as a monad fetching thought from some remote unknown. The *Visions* reminds us of *The Clod and the Pebble* because of the parallel with Theotormon and Bromion and also because of the image of the stream, applied by Oothoon to herself. This image, as we have seen on pp. 119–22, shows that the conceptions of life produced by clod and pebble are impoverished ones – they see themselves as incomplete beings, each lacking the functions of the other. Oothoon is compared to a spring in such a way that she is seen to have the functions of both clod and pebble and, because she integrates the functions, to have a nature that is quite different. Oothoon calls on the 'kings of the sounding air' to rend away her bosom so that she may reflect the image of Theotormon, at which:

> Theotormon severely smiles. her soul reflects the smile;
> As the clear spring mudded with feet of beasts grows pure & smiles.

> (Pl. 2, l. 18)

Like the clod, the stream can take an impression, it can be 'mudded with feet of beasts', but like the pebble it has a nature and organization of its own and regains its own character. The stream is capable of reception but modifies what is received without making a submissive copy in the manner of the clod. Unlike the pebble, the spring is not self-contained but is a reflection of its surroundings. Its transparency would render it invisible if it did not take its colour from elsewhere. In the case of the stream, perception is a form of organization and organization is a kind of perception. It is not self-sufficient nor is it servile, neither tyrant nor slave, but must be what it is in order to take other things into account, and must take other things into account in order to be what it is. The life of the stream is not one of set ways, but one of organized renewal and a prolonged youthfulness of vision.

Theotormon is a figure of gloomy guiltiness. His horror of the sexual act, his punishment of the guilty pair, the restrictions he places on himself, his self-torturings, his jealousy, his slave-owning, his unbending strictness, the morbid satisfaction he takes in ideas of corruption and retributive justice, his self-absorption, his abhorrence of the life of the senses, and his strictly rational approach, are all characteristic of the austere religiosity attributed to him by Oothoon:

> Why dost thou seek religion?
> Is it because acts are not lovely, that thou seekest solitude,
> Where the horrible darkness is impressed with reflections of
>   desire.
>
> (Pl. 7, l. 9)

Even Theotormon's name threatens us with God's wrath and with rigid reasonings about man's duty. Clearly, his god would be the tyrant in the skies favoured by those branches of nearly all religions that dwell self-righteously on guilt. He is the god of a chosen people who countenances wholesale executions of the erring and is addressed by Oothoon as 'Urizen! Creator of men! mistaken Demon of heaven' (Pl. 5, l.3). Towards the end of the poem she anathematizes him:

> Father of Jealousy. be thou accursed from the earth!
> Why hast thou taught my Theotormon this accursed thing?
> Till beauty fades from off my shoulders darken'd and cast
>   out,
> A solitary shadow wailing on the margin of non-entity.
>
> (Pl. 7, l. 12)

197

Theotormon's position is shown as even more distasteful if we accept that he and Bromion are aspects of the same person, a man composed, not of desires and satisfactions, but of lusts and restrictions. As Bromion, he rapes his wife Oothoon, and as Theotormon he makes both Oothoon and himself suffer in revulsion at what they have done. Oothoon describes the life of the wife and children of such a man, ridden with guilt, though unable to restrain himself, and imposing furtive guiltiness on others:

>   and she must drag the chain
> Of life in weary lust; must chilling, murderous thoughts obscure
> The clear heaven of her eternal spring! to bear the wintry rage
> Of a harsh terror driv'n to madness, bound to hold a rod
> Over her shrinking shoulders all the day: & all the night
> To turn the wheel of false desire: and longings that wake her womb
> To the abhorred birth of cherubs in the human form
> That live a pestilence & die a meteor & are no more.
> Till the child dwell with one he hates, and do the deed he loaths
> And the impure scourge force his seed into its unripe birth
> E'er yet his eyelids can behold the arrows of the day.
>
>   (Pl. 5, l. 22)

Theotormon and Bromion cannot combine to form a complete man – they can only torture each other – though in a divided being a Theotormon is, of course, necessary, for if appetites have become destructive it is well that they should be restrained. Oothoon, on the other hand, is complete and gives her motives different names. The 'lust' of Bromion is her 'desire' and the 'jealousy' of Theotormon her 'love'.

Theotormon is associated with the faculty of abstract thought, a faculty which he misuses by allowing it to dominate his life. His reasonings are distorted, unlike those of Oothoon who can think to good purpose because her mental powers are integrated with

other faculties, and who spends her time attempting to persuade
Theotormon that there are depths to his mind, though he insists
on ignoring them. She argues by analogy, showing how all
creatures obey the dictates of their nature, their 'pursuits' being
'as different as their forms and as their joys' (Pl. 3, l. 6). Men too,
she argues, are guided, not only by rational principles, but also by
their personal inclinations which give colour to their reasonings:
'How can the giver of gifts experience the delights of the merchant?' she asks (Pl. 5, l. 12). Theotormon overlooks these rather
obvious facts and hypostatizes thought, attempting to find some
home for it more permanent than the changeable human consciousness. He sees ideas as composed of archetypes, not as
existentially determined:

> Where goest thou O thought! to what remote land is thy
>   flight!
> If thou returnest to the present moment of affliction
> Wilt thou bring comforts on thy wings and dews and honey
>   and balm;
> Or poison from the desart wilds. from the eyes of the
>   envier.
>
> (Pl. 4, l. 8)

Theotormon demeans his rational powers because his attempt to
provide reason with too absolute a basis is an outcome of dogmatism, a rigidity which is unreasonable. The success of the
rational mind should be measured by the width of its view, by its
ability to work with a world continually in flux, to abide by its
own principles in its intercourse with that world and yet modify
those principles intelligently and benevolently. Because Theotormon wishes to maintain his principles unchanged he insists
that they are unconditioned and he severs communication with a
world that might threaten them. Perhaps it is because Theotormon's thoughts leave the earth seeking a more rarefied atmosphere
that they are associated, in the *Visions*, with eagles. Oothoon calls
on the eagles to 'Rend away this defiled bosom' (Pl.2, l. 15). At
this stage she is prepared to repent and attempt the agony of

contrition approved of by him. He displays the only sign of emotion that is not centred completely on himself when he 'severely smiles' (Pl. 2, l. 18), though it is evident that the gratification he feels at seeing 'justice' done is sadistic. Oothoon attempts to persuade herself that Theotormon's reasonings are correct and allows his eagles to rend her fleshly garments. These are birds of night, unnaturally hunting where nothing can be seen. They forage in the dark regions of Theotormon's mind, though eagles, like the intellect, belong properly to the light and with width of vision. Theoromon's reasonings, like his conception of reason itself, are distorted, and though Oothoon attempts, for love of the man, to judge herself by his standards, her own reasoning seeks the day and she sees that she is innocent:

> the Eagle returns
> From nightly prey, and lifts his golden beak to the pure
> east;
> Shaking the dust from his immortal pinions to awake
> The sun that sleeps too long. Arise my Theotormon I am
> pure.
> Because the night is gone that clos'd me in its deadly black.
>
> (Pl. 2, l. 25)

Theotormon's intellect is used to enclose him more deeply in his gloomy dogma, but Oothoon uses hers to give herself wings and vision. Because she is in touch with her world and is aware of the complexity of her being, she cannot be satisfied with any formula which too readily explains her human nature:

> They told me that I had five senses to inclose me up.
> And they inclos'd my infinite brain into a narrow circle.
> And sunk my heart into the Abyss, a red round globe hot
> burning
> Till all from life I was obliterated and erased.
>
> (Pl. 2, l. 31)

Sensationalist and rationalist doctrines of the mind, both of which are indicated here, come to much the same thing, being descriptive of a limited mode of being, though they successfully describe limited creatures like Bromium and Theotormon. Oothoon rejects the inadequate formula and rejects also Theotormon's inadequate morality. There is no further talk, on her part, of mortification of the flesh or expiation of sin. Because her soul is complete she has no lusts – only desires which are holy – and no sins – only the enjoyments of her mind and body which are pure. She is:

> Open to joy and to delight where ever beauty appears
> If in the morning sun I find it: there my eyes are fix'd
> In happy copulation; if in evening mild, wearied with work;
> Sit on a bank and draw the pleasures of this free born joy.
>
> (Pl. 6, l. 22)

Although Oothoon has resolved the moral question to her satisfaction, however, she can never find fulfilment unless she can bring Theotormon to his senses too. During the remainder of the poem she persists in a vain attempt to lead him intellectually to a position for which he is psychologically unfitted. Her truths cannot be valid for him and he allots her a position bound to his animal part because he can only regard her freedom as bestial. Those who are without Oothoon's vitality will deny her its enjoyment and regard her as wanton because she does not conform to their limited ideas. Theotormon is isolated because he has lost his means of communication, and Oothoon is also alone because those she speaks to cannot hear or understand her. Only the Daughters of Albion 'hear her woes, & eccho back her sighs'.

Like the Daughters of Jerusalem in the Song of Solomon, the Daughters of Albion are sympathetic to Oothoon in her search for her lover. The name 'Albion' given these kindred souls, who are apparently in a predicament similar to Oothoon's, is best explained by considering the poem at its political level. Oothoon is 'the soft soul of America', the representative of a country which had recently revolted, thrown off an old authority and gained the opportunity of making a new start. At the time that the *Visions* was

was being etched (1793) the Revolution, so it was claimed, had given France a similar opportunity to establish brotherhood and liberty in place of prejudice and repression as the guiding principles of a new state. If Theotormon, as puritanical husband, puts moral gyves on his household, then as conservative ruler he puts legal gyves on the freedom of thought and opportunity of the subjects he governs. Oothoon, the daughter of the American and French Revolutions, is not free, because she cannot get her new governors to adopt methods other than those of restriction based on the assumption that all men are potential law-breakers – the assumption that human nature is evil and needs strict control. In other words, the methods of the new rulers are those of the pre-revolutionary masters. The Daughters of Albion, the daughters of the industrial revolution in England, can sympathize with the daughter of America. Their old woes – laws to control movement, wages and speech – are recognized as the woes of the new states where the same repressions are being applied in the same spirit as before.

Oothoon pleads with Theotormon to accept her new vision, the outcome of daylight reasoning, in place of the rigid dogma which elaborates itself within his closed and darkened mind. Her plea is partly a passionate statement of her love, of her hopes and convictions, and partly an attempt to convince her lover that his psychological and epistemological notions are wrong. On the one hand there are such declarations as: 'I am white and pure to hover round Theotormons breast' (Pl.3, l. 20), and 'I cry, Love! Love! Love! happy happy Love! free as the mountain wind!' (Pl. 7, l. 16). On the other hand are long harangues in which question after question is asked in an attempt to shake Theotormon's theory of the isolation of the mind. It is appropriate, of course, that Oothoon should make the theoretical approach. She is representative of the rational emancipated womankind Mary Wollstonecraft hoped for but she knows, also, that if Theotormon's mind is accessible at all, it is so only to abstruse argument. A further reason for this approach, a reason that somewhat diminishes the *Visions* as a work of art, is that Oothoon is acting obviously as the mouthpiece of Blake who is making an attack on the moral philosophies of the eighteenth century, and the reader is aware of her in this rôle.

The didactic purpose of the poem becomes rather obtrusive.

The chief strength of Oothoon's attack lies in its comprehensiveness. Theotormon, being a divided mind, has more than one theory to express his loneliness, just as the eighteenth century had more than one mode of indicating the barrier between mind and universe. For Oothoon these theories all come to very much the same thing because they are all indicative of a condition she regards as undesirable – the self-centred habit of mind which gives rise to the theories and lends them probability when stated.

On plates 3 and 4 Theotormon puts forward his argument, first questioning the substantial reality of mental processes, though this, as we soon see, is only in order to ascribe to them another, more mysterious 'reality':

> Tell me what is a thought? & of what substance is it made?
> Tell me what is a joy? & in what gardens do joys grow?
>
> (Pl. 3, l. 23)

His queries are rather absurd and he goes on, just as absurdly, to give thoughts a permanent and rigid form. They are not called up from moment to moment by the mind in relation to the circumstances of the thinker, but are archetypal and come from some remote unknown to displace each other in the solitary awareness of the individual:

> Tell me where dwell the thoughts forgotten till thou
> call them forth
> Tell me where dwell the joys of old! & where the
> ancient loves!
> And when will they renew again & the night of
> oblivion past?
>
> (Pl. 4, l. 4)

Theotormon is aware only of his thoughts as they come fully formed from a 'remote land' (Pl. 4, l. 8), but he knows also that they are sent, occasionally to comfort him, more often to torment him, by some mysterious being he refers to as 'the envier' (Pl. 4, l.11). His 'present moment of affliction' (Pl. 4, l. 9) is ordained else-where and comes to him ready made, as it were. His emotion does not arise in response to anything.

Theotormon asserts that the subjective workings of his mind are absolute, while Bromion questions the substantial reality of the objective world. Bromion's answer made in opposition to Theo-tormon (Pl. 4, ll.13–24) asserts that though it is possible to make statements about the 'objects' that inhabit one's mind, one cannot regard these 'perceptions' as bearing a significant relationship to phenomena:

> And is there not eternal fire and eternal chains?
> To bind the phantoms of existence from eternal life?
>
> (Pl. 4, l. 23)

It is possible to 'know' one's own sensations, but to assume know-ledge of a reality giving rise to those sensations is to claim too much. We cannot know anything about what we call 'reality' and we know nothing about the sensations of other beings:

> Thou knowest that the ancient trees seen by thine
>   eyes have fruit;
> But knowest thou that trees and fruits flourish upon
>   the earth
> To gratify senses unknown? trees beasts and birds
>   unknown
>
> (Pl. 4, l. 13)

We know only the kaleidoscope presented to us by our own senses, and so our emotions (unlike Theotormon's) are an outcome of immediate sensation (though these sensations are not demon-strably *of* anything):

> are there other sorrows, beside the sorrows of poverty?
> And are there other joys, beside the joys of riches and ease?
>
> (Pl. 4, l. 20)

Theotormon's idea of a universe governed by the arbitrary dictates of the 'envier' is also denied and Bromion postulates, instead, the impartial control of rigid laws: 'is there not one law for both the lion and the ox?' (Pl. 4, l. 22). A knowledge of these laws is derived, presumably, by making a study of one's sensations.

It is unnecessary to trace the implications of Theotormon's and Bromion's philosophies in detail – indeed that would be to miss the point that their mental labour is futile. Theotormon is a rationalist who owes something to Plato and not a little to Descartes and Leibniz. Bromion is a sensationalist, indebted to Locke and Berkeley, Blake's two quasi-philosophers speak only twenty-seven lines between them but they manage to give an outline, in that space, of the sort of problem that engrossed the eighteenth century, though these speakers have no philosophic detachment whatever. Their arguments are too cryptic, vague and one-sided to be taken very seriously, but they are interesting for the following reasons. First, their apparently contradictory statements have a good deal in common. Second, they are of importance as revealing the mentality of the speaker rather than as establishing epistemological truths or falsehoods. Third, Oothoon has anticipated their arguments and, by implication, proved them inadequate.

Bromion states that human awareness is composed of fleeting sensations and he could, no doubt, go on to enunciate the laws of association which give these sensations stability and regularity. But these sensations are not necessarily perceptions in the normal sense of the word. They are private internal elaborations, regular enough, but made regular by mental process, not by correspondence with regularities in the phenomenal universe. If Bromion says that his mind works in this way he may be right. Only he knows what goes on within himself. What is of interest here is that he is not saying anything different from Theotormon. Both men insist that their mental processes are self-contained, but the one calls these processes 'thoughts', the other calls them 'sensations'. Neither man, however, says anything to indicate that the difference is other than a terminological one. They have different explanations for these processes it is true, Theotormon stating that they are controlled by God, Bromion that 'law' controls them, but these are hypothetical elaborations, and the elaborations are similar. A vaguely hostile god and an inexorable blind law amount to much the same thing – very little is known of either, both are beyond one's control, and both impose an uncomfortable order on the isolated consciousness. The metaphysical theories of Theotormon and Bromion differ in detail and in the labels they use, but are basically very similar. They are not of interest because they state any ultimate truth, but because they reveal the mental condition of the speaker. Because they are isolated, self-willed creatures it is necessary for them to postulate theories that account for their state, and a human being not limited in their way, as Oothoon is less limited, would put forward a different theory. The tyrant determined to impose his will yet wishing to avoid responsibility, often claims to be acting on behalf of some god or some force greater than himself, and Theotormon and Bromion postulate such controlling agents. The tyrant is insensitive to the needs and purposes of others and the solipsistic theories of the two men are a just reflection of their lack of awareness.

The theories of Theotormon and Bromion represent the philosophies of the Enlightenment in the form of a caricature, the object of which is not to suggest that the theories of Bacon, Locke or Berkeley are so much claptrap, but to regret that they should be necessary. The theories are true because they are evolved to explain what we are – beings in some degrees of solitude: the more total the isolation, the more extreme the theoretical statement that testifies to it. We derive our notions of the human condition by observing ourselves, though it is not reasonable to assume that such notions are universally applicable. Solitude is not the only possible state (as Oothoon vainly argues) though the solitary state is selfish, involves a sense of guilt, and attempts to lessen that sense by declaring all men similarly guilty; Theotormon cannot afford to pay attention to Oothoon's argument because he has an interest in supposing that his description of man is the only true one. And his theory, evolved to explain his condition, has the effect of inveterately establishing him in it.

Oothoon opposes the philosophy of Bromion and Theotormon because it is not true for her and because it need not be true for them if they could undergo a change of heart. She anticipates their arguments:

> They told me that the night & day were all that I could see;
> They told me that I had five senses to inclose me up.
> And they inclos'd my infinite brain into a narrow circle.
> And sunk my heart into the Abyss, a red round globe hot burning
> Till all from life I was obliterated and erased.
>
> (Pl. 2, l. 30)

Oothoon is objecting to the statements of Theotormon and Bromion, which are reminiscent of theories she has heard before – reminiscent, for instance, of a celebrated passage in Hume, the philosopher who brings rationalist and sensationalist theories together:

> For my part, when I enter most intimately into what I call *myself*, I always stumble on some particular perception or other, of heat or cold, light or shade, love or hatred, pain or pleasure. I never can catch *myself* at any time without a perception, and never can observe anything but the perception. When my perceptions are removed for any time, as by sound sleep, so long am I insensible of *myself*, and may truly be said not to exist . . . The mind is a kind of theatre, where several perceptions successively make their appearance; pass, repass, glide away, and mingle in an infinite variety of postures and situations. There is properly no *simplicity* in it at one time, nor *identity* in different, whatever natural propension we may have to imagine that simplicity and identity. The comparison of the theatre must not mislead us. They are the successive perceptions only, that constitute the mind; nor have we the most distant notion of the place where these scenes are represented, or of the materials of which it is composed.
>
> (*Treatise*, I, iv, 6)

Oothoon claims that she has been undervalued and thwarted by the application of a doctrine very similar to that of Hume. As the doctrine is enunciated by the two men in the *Visions*, it is Bromion who states it in terms most nearly resembling Hume's, though both Bromion and Theotormon are substantially in agreement, as we have seen. Like Hume, they see the mind as a theatre where unreal ghostly fancies display themselves, and like Hume they relinquish a knowledge of the 'place' of representation (the world) and the 'materials' which compose it, and relinquish the notion of *simplicity* and *identity* in the mind (the soul). Where Hume seems slightly uneasy in stating his doctrine, uneasy because he must do so in the face of common belief and his own 'natural propension' (common sense), Bromion and Theotormon are in despair at the loss of their world and of their continued 'identity'. Bromion makes his 'lamentation' for the 'phantoms of existence' (Pl. 4, l. 24), and Theotormon's 'secret tears' are shed for his life, which is a 'night of oblivion' (Pl. 4, l. 5). Oothoon is not troubled as they are, though not because she retains the simple faith they mourn. A completed soul and a rigid universe can only clash with each other, and Oothoon describes a world and soul which exist in bringing each other to fulfilment. Bromion and Theotormon are in despair because they find the world and the soul less substantial, less separate and less definite than they think these things ought to be, but Oothoon can live happily while accepting such terms of existence. She asserts that the world can only come to the individual as he allows it to, though that is no reason for denying the world in despair, with Theotormon. On the other hand, the thoughts and actions of the individual are given their final shape by experience, instructing him through his senses, though that is no reason for abandoning the notion of individuality with Bromion. Bromion and Theotormon have discovered that the 'great Globe' is an 'insubstantial pageant' and that 'we are such stuff as dreams are made on', and are so dissatisfied with their discovery that they cannot pay attention to the splendours of the pageant or the excitement of the dream. Oothoon attempts to rally them by pointing out that nothing is absolute and that all things pass away. This condition must be accepted so that we may turn our attention to the 'dream', no less important because it must fade:

Does not the worm erect a pillar in the mouldering churchyard?
And a palace of eternity in the jaws of the hungry grave
Over his porch these words are written. Take thy bliss O man!
And sweet shall be thy taste & sweet thy infant joys renew!

(Pl. 5, l. 41)

In impermanence we may be triumphant, as the worm is, which
erects its 'pillar' as a suitably transitory monument, and in wel-
coming man to death exhorts him to life. Oothoon is triumphant,
but fails to comfort Theotormon, who continues to reject life
because he cannot tolerate the notion of death.

It is inevitable that Theotormon and Bromion should separate
to become a divided mind. The one denies real identity to the
knower while the other denies substantial reality to what is known.
They would find it awkward to maintain the two positions simultaneously because, together, they negate the whole of experience,
or so they would suppose. Oothoon takes their arguments further,
implying that if the dreamer is the dream, reality an image we
create, and the self we long to find a creation of time, then it does
not follow that nothing of significance is present, or that nothing
of value can be found. Bromion and Theotormon are in despair
because they cannot discover the absolute reality and identity that
only a bad habit of looking for fictions has caused them to require,
and the search for these fictions has prevented them from enjoying
the difficult 'reality' that blurs the boundaries between knower and
known. This would not matter if they could enjoy a satisfactory
life while in search of these fictions, but the fact that they are intent on finding them is indicative of an unhealthy condition. They
would like to be confronted with fixed entities so that they could
deal with life categorically, without real or responsible thinking.
Dogma and prejudice flourish in the mind which can take the world
unimaginatively, while the mind that is prepared to encounter a
more demanding world, to which it is organically related, is
obliged to maintain elasticity in its values. Theotormon and Bromion would like to live in a world of ultimate things and fixed
laws while Oothoon is open to experience, and takes things as they
come:

209

How can one joy absorb another? are not different joys
Holy, eternal infinite? and each joy is a Love.

(Pl. 5, l. 5)

Eternity is to be found, not in an indefinite prolongation of any
experience, but in a quality of enjoyment which allows a relaxa-
tion of the sense of time. Blake expresses a similar idea in the fragment *Eternity* (discussed on pages 43–4, and 15):

> He who bends to himself a joy
> Does the winged life destroy;
> But he who kisses the joy as it flies
> Lives in Eternity's sun rise.

Theotormon's anxiety for permanent satisfactions ensures that
he can know none, while Oothoon, who has no desire to force
things, can receive what joys are to be had. Blake's illustration to
the 'Argument' of the *Visions* depicts Oothoon kissing a joy as it
flies. The joy, as a nymph, is rising in flight from the 'Marygold of
Leutha's vale'. Oothoon bends forward to kiss it on the lips, but
without making any attempt to grasp at it, while behind the pair
the rays of the sun rise above the horizon. The nymph of the
Marygold urges Oothoon:

> pluck thou my flower Oothoon the mild
> Another flower shall spring. because the soul of sweet delight
> Can never pass away.

(Pl. 1, l. 8)

Delights, like flowers, may pass away, and indeed they must if
they grow from a living soul which retains its capacity for delight.
A selfish attempt to force delights into being or to prolong them
can only make them ugly. Primarily the Marygold stands for the
delight of sexual experience, which must be unselfish and spontaneous if it is to be properly enjoyed, but Blake is referring us to
all delights, which must be surrendered if they are to flower again.
Oothoon describes joys as 'infants' (Pl. 8, l. 9) always new born,
and describes herself as 'Open to joy and to delight where ever

beauty appears' (Pl. 6, l. 22). Her love is unselfish, while the love of Theotormon is an envious 'self-love' that:

> drinks another as a sponge drinks water!
> That clouds with jealousy his nights, with weepings all the day:
> To spin a web of age around him, grey and hoary! dark!
> Till his eyes sicken at the fruit that hangs before his sight.
>
> (Pl. 7, l. 17)

The joys of Oothoon are 'infant' and 'winged', they are lively and come and go as they please, while the corresponding emotions in Theotormon are lusts – tantalizing fruits that cannot be eaten and cannot be ignored.

Theotormon and Bromion put forward their arguments in an obscure abstract manner while Oothoon answers them by citing examples which, she hopes, they will think about, and so persuade themselves that they are wrong. Her method carries its own lesson. Because Theotormon and Bromion confine themselves to abstractions they are led to giving their terms a spurious value. They use the words, 'senses' and 'thought' as though they stood for essences, to be discussed without reference to a specific mind or specific occasion. Oothoon uses the words realistically and attempts to correct the two men by alluding to diversities of sensation and thought. What is known depends on the instincts and character of the knower as well as on the realm of his knowing:

> With what sense does the bee form cells? have not
>   the mouse & frog
> Eyes and ears and sense of touch? yet are their
>   habitations
> And their pursuits as different as their forms and
>   as their joys.
>
> (Pl. 3, l. 4)

Sensing and living are very different activities in different species and man has his own qualities:

ask the rav'nous snake
Where she gets poison: & the wing'd eagle why he loves the sun
And then tell me the thoughts of man. that have been hid of old.

(Pl. 3, l. 11)

We have a human nature which loves thought, just as the eagle loves the sun, so, though our thoughts need to be developed by experience, we don't acquire them passively, but actively and individually create them. Bromion and Theotormon misuse their abstractions so as to over-simplify their account of life, postulating mechanical relationships in place of living ones. They are so busy lamenting the loss of the world that they fail to see that the world waits to be created, though they, like all other men, must make the effort to create it:

How can the giver of gifts experience the delights of the merchant?
How the industrious citizen the pains of the husbandman.
....
How different their eye and ear! how different the world to them!

(Pl. 5, l. 12)

'Reality', what is known, gets some of its attributes from the condition of being known. Theotormon, however, supposes that all attributes are supplied by the knower, and therefore despairs of the world. 'Mind', on the other hand, receives some of its attributes from experience – from what is known. But Bromion despairs of mind, assuming that it is the sum of its 'perceptions'. Both men have a mania for simple and uncontaminated categories: pure thought and pure sensation which they believe in; pure soul and pure reality which they cannot believe in, but the loss of which obsesses them. Oothoon attempts to bring them to their senses:

Sweetest the fruit that the worm feeds on. & the
    soul prey'd on by woe
The new wash'd lamb ting'd with the village smoke &
    the bright swan
By the red earth of our immortal river.   (Pl. 3, l. 17)

Purity of the sort they desire would be insipid if it occurred, but it doesn't, and their desire for it misleads them, not only in their metaphysical speculations (which do not matter very much) but also in their moral attitudes (which do matter). Oothoon would not attempt to convince the two men that the subjective and objective aspects of experience cannot be disentangled if she did not wish them to realize that their preoccupation with purity causes them to set up false expectations of life. Theotormon finds that he has sexual impulses, together with the animals, and because he cannot be an angel he despairs of being anything but an animal. Sexually, he cannot be a human being, and Blake depicts him without genitals. In one illustration he is seen scourging himself. He takes the gloomiest view of human nature because human motives are mixed. Like all selfists he has found that there is an element of selfishness in the make-up of man, so concludes that selfishness makes up the whole, and all men, including himself, must suffer under his disapprobation. Oothoon who can view herself in all her complexity can take a delight in her activities without hypocrisy, and without hiding one half of her life from the other as Theotormon (Bromion) is forced to do.

INDEX TO POEMS